SOMEBODY TOLD THE TRUTH

Selected Lyrics and Stories

PETER CASE

Boom & Chime Books • 2020

"On the Way to Daly City" originally appeared in *Your Golden Sun Still Shines: San Francisco Personal Histories and Small Fictions*

Boom and Chime Books
5758 Geary Blvd. #365
San Francisco, CA 94121

www.petercase.com

Illustrations by the author

Layout by Kelly Dessaint

Distributed by Phony Lid Books

ISBN: 978-1-930935-45-7

First printing, October 2020

For Denise

Books by Peter Case

As Far As You Can Get Without A Passport
(Everthemore books, 2006)

Epistolary Rex
(with David Ensminger, Left of the Dial, 2011)

Subterranean Hum
(with David Ensminger, Left of the Dial, 2014)

"All words are spiritual. Nothing is more spiritual than words." —Walt Whitman

"The mote spar disappears and you have three eyes" —Alice Notley, Benediction

Contents

SOMEBODY TOLD THE TRUTH

Just Hangin' On

Smiling salutations from a soldier boy
Dressed in blue denim and corduroy
They don't care what you say
If you talk fast they'll listen anyway

They're just hangin' on
They're just hangin' on

Since I was born I've been fighting time
I see the time passing and it eases my mind
That's not the way I should feel
Watching the clock makes it all unreal

I'm just hangin' on
I'm just hangin' on
I'm just hangin' on

Everyone around me is at their ends
Running from their enemies and crying to their friends
It's got me thinking of why I'm so lonely
And I'm calling it love

I'm just hangin' on
I'm just hangin' on
I'm just hangin' on
I'm just hangin' on

1970; The Midnight Broadcast, 2020

When You Find Out

I try to explain what you don't see
No one can give you more love than me
You say you're waiting for just the right one
You'll try to find me when he lets you down
When you find out I was the one
When you find out I was the one

This is the last time I'm gonna try
I still want you but I'll say goodbye
You say you're waiting for just the right one
You'll try to find me when he lets you down
When you find out I was the one
When you find out I was the one

I'll be gone
When you find out
It's gonna be pretty hard on you
I'll be gone
When you find out
I hope there's still something you can do

This is the last time I'm gonna try
I still want you but I'll say goodbye
You say you're waiting for just the right one
You'll try to find me when he lets you down
When you find out I was the one
When you find out I was the one

I'll be gone
When you find out
It's gonna be pretty hard on you
I'll be gone
When you find out
I hope there's still something you can do

This is the last time I'm gonna try
I still want you but I'll say goodbye
You say you're waiting for just the right one
You'll try to find me when he lets you down
When you find out I was the one
When you find out I was the one
When you find out
When you find out
When you find out
When you find out

1974; The Nerves EP, 1976

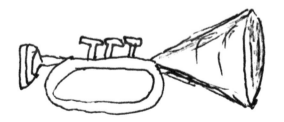

Zero Hour

The bells are ringing
Girl, it's getting late
The train's pulling out
There's no time to waste, now
You better move fast
You better move fast

Staple your ticket
And put on your shoes
Pack up your suitcase
There's no time to lose, now
You better move fast
You better move fast

It's getting late now it's time to go
It's over the top now it's out of control
It's just a matter or time
Until the zero hour
Until the zero hour

The lights are shining get out of that bed
The phone is ringing but it's gone to your head, now
Yeah, you better move fast
You better move fast

It's time to look at what you've done
It's time to finish all you've begun, now
You better move fast
You better move fast

It's getting late now it's time to go
It's over the top now it's out of control
Its just a matter or time
Until the zero hour
Until the zero hour

It's getting late now it's time to go
It's over the top now it's out of control
Its just a matter or time
Until the zero hour
Until the zero hour

Until the zero hour
Until the zero

Zero Hour, 1980

In This Town

From the day I got here, I could never see clear
    in this town
I had nothing to show, no place to go
    in this town
Where the gravity pulls down twice as strong
Twenty-four hours takes twice as long
In this town

Saturday night we go ride the range
    in this town
Driving 'round looking for some kind of change
    in this town
Where the things I need are all sold out
No one even knows what I'm talking about
In this town

In this town is there someone
To talk to me and let me know?
Don't make me wait, are you out there?
I can't see you anywhere

In this town our life goes on
We stay right here and we just hang on
All you gotta do is take a look around
In this town

The Plimsouls, 1981

A Million Miles Away

Friday night, I just got back
I had my eyes shut
Was dreaming about the past
Thought about you while the radio played
Should have got moving
Some reason I stayed
I started drifting to a different place
Realized I was falling off the face of your world
And there was nothing there to bring me back

I'm a million miles away
A million miles away
Just a million miles away
And there's nothing left to bring me back today

I took a ride and went downtown
Streets were empty, there was no one around
All the faces that we used to know
Gone from the places we used to go
I'm at the wrong end of your looking glass
Trying to hold onto the hands of the past and you
And there's nothing left to bring me back

I'm a million miles away
A million miles away
Just a million miles away
And there's nothing left to bring me back today
Bring me back today

I'm at the wrong end of your looking glass
Trying to hold onto the hands of the past and you
And there's nothing left to bring me back

I'm a million miles away
A million miles away
A million miles away
And there's nothing left to bring me back today
Bring me back today
Bring me back today
Bring me back today

(Peter Case, Joey Alkes, Chris Fradkin)

Shaky City/Bomp single, 1982

Oldest Story In The World

It makes perfect sense
Seeing how the seeds were sown
To find you out there on your own
You said your goodbyes
    and broke all the ties
It struck me dumb
    to think I tried for you

Tonight you can feel the seasons
    changing
You'll never change
Though you're no better
    than the weather
You're cool but there's rain
    in your heart
You're blown like a feather

That's the oldest story in the world
You lost the key to paradise
That's the oldest story in the world

Did we have it made?
Somehow I thought we could remain
If nothing lasts no one's to blame
And you can't look back
To where you we got off the track
That's a mystery that we'll never crack

It's just the oldest story in the world
We lost the key to paradise
That's the oldest story in the world
Someday we gotta to set it right
And that's the oldest story in the world
You'll hear it again and again

That's the oldest story in the world, yeah

Somehow I thought we could remain
If nothing lasts no one's to blame
And you can't look back
    to where we got off the track
That's a mystery that we'll never crack

It's just the oldest story in the world
Lost the key to paradise
That's the oldest story in the world
Someday we gotta set it right
That's the oldest story in the world
Just like a rolling stone
That's the oldest story, that's the oldest story
Now you can't go home
And that's the oldest story in the world

"Well, I don't want to leave but it's time to go"
"Where?"
"Well, I just don't know"
And that's the oldest story in the world

Everywhere At Once, 1983

I Shook His Hand

I was a kid out behind the fair
His words were like lightning in the summer air
His eyes were wild with the truth he told
Holding back the rain while the thunder rolled
Too young not to understand
I was proud to say I shook his hand
I shook his hand

He took command on a winter's day
And all across the land spring was on its way
He struck fear into the hearts of fools
Raking up the gangs, breaking all their rules
Too young not to understand
I was proud to say I shook his hand
I shook his hand

Each tongue is a world, each eye is an ocean
Of every man, woman, child here in living motion
Now, who will protect us, who will perfect us?
Oh, who will live to see the day when love connects us?
Who'll take a step out in this land?
I'd be proud to say I shook his hand
I shook his hand

For years they tried to kill him, he finally died
I still remember how I felt while my mama cried
I grew up with a bullet in my breast
If you know it or not, so did all the rest
Too young not to understand
I was proud to say I shook his hand
I shook his hand

Each tongue is a world, each eye is an ocean
Of every man, woman, child here in living motion
Now, who will protect us, who will perfect us?
Oh, who will live to see the day when love connects us?
Who'd take a step out in this land?
I'd be proud to say I shook his hand

I shook his hand
Well, I shook his hand
I shook his hand
I shook his hand

Peter Case, 1986

Trusted Friend

The shades are drawn, the lines are too
It's just me and you, my trusted friend
Heavy steps, it's a burden I can tell
I heard you hesitate before you rang the bell
My trusted friend—straight to the end

When you walked in I was searching through a trunk
Trying to separate the memories from the junk
Now your confession leaves my vision blurred
How do I know what to keep—listening to your words?
My trusted friend—straight to the end

That I've seen before
Night pouring out of your eyes
Leaning by my door
Saying your goodbyes
Like nothing's going to change
It's going to be the same
Oh, don't go yet, my trusted friend

My knees are shaking and my palms begin to sweat
Oh, don't go yet my trusted friend
Wait, tomorrow, we'll see it in the light
It's just emotions running blacker than the night
My trusted friend—straight to the end

That I've seen before
Night pouring out of your eyes
Leaning by my door
Saying your goodbyes
Like nothing's going to change
It's going to be the same
Oh, don't go yet, my trusted friend

1984, The Case Files, 2011

Walk in the Woods

Out past the cemetery, down by the willow bend
Half a mile from the railroad track
Last seen together, these two lovers hand in hand
Took a walk in the woods and they never come back
They took a walk in the woods and they never come back

Metal from the radio, it rang out through the fields
Just when they thought they'd found the track
Through a patch of four leaf clover that vanished in
    thin air
They took a walk in the woods and they never come back
They took a walk in the woods and they never come back

Never before in history has this town been so up in arms
You never heard such misery as those bloodhounds 'cross
    the farms
Between God and the police they were protected from
    all harm
Until they walked in the woods and they never come back
They took a walk in the woods and they never come back
They never come back
They never come back

Sirens wailed emergency, no evidence was removed
You never heard such theories, but none of them could
    be proved
For the missing children, no conscience could be soothed
They took a walk in the woods and they never come back

Well, that was fifteen years ago, I guess we've come a long,
    long way
I never heard the end of it, you know, I couldn't stay
When I'm not stuck for time or money, I still wonder
    'bout that day

I took a walk in the woods and I never come back
I took a walk in the woods and I never come back
I never come back
I never come back
I took a walk in the woods and I never come back

Peter Case, 1986

Ice Water

All kinds of people want all kinds of things
Some want money, some want diamond rings
I fell in love in with a millionaire's daughter
People in hell want ice water

Well, I asked for her hand, she said, "Go see my pa"
I found him in the garden, said, "I'll be your son-in-law"
Even showed him the thirty-dollar ring that I bought her
He said, "People in hell want ice water"

Back under her window I pulled out my rope
I said, "Come on down here, honey, and we'll elope"
She climbed halfway, fell the rest and I caught her
The sky was black and it rained ice water

Now, the millionaire's daughter and me are living in a shack
I work the mill all day, at night she dreams of going back
I try to remember the first time I saw her
And the people in hell want ice water

Well, I try to remember the first time I saw her
And the people in hell want ice water

(Peter Case, Sam Hopkins)

Peter Case, 1986

Small Town Spree

Saw you smiling from the front page of this morning's paper
Looking sharp as alibis for your latest caper
A look in your eyes I never thought I'd see
The captain said you'd been arrested in connection
    with the small town spree

Said you broke down on your way out to New York City
Snow was on the ground, the moonlight must've looked
    so pretty
Abandoned your car not far from the last bar you'd see
Where you lied to the people inside and tried to hide
    after your small town spree

It all started at Gate's Liquor Store
You helped yourself to a bottle of scotch
Strolled down to Miller's Drugs
Forged a check and borrowed a watch
Bells were ringing at St. Peter and Paul's
When you stole the collection box
In the night a violent wind tore the silence of the
    farmhouse where you fired the shots

I remember one December morning when we were
    younger
Jenny drinking tea while you spoke to her and me
    with eyes of wonder
You two were so in love then—I never thought I'd be
Looking one morning at the story in the paper of your
    small town spree
Looking at the story of your small town spree

Peter Case, 1986

Steel Strings

Well, all those nights they hit rock bottom
The songs they sang, well, we forgot 'em
You could hear them play with shaky hands
Guitars strung up with rubber bands
Singing, do you want a man of steel, or
Do you want a man that's real?
They used to play in the courts of kings
Now, they're only made of steel
    when they're on steel strings

They used to be on every schoolgirl's wall
And they never dropped the beat at all
They could make it soar, they could make it hop
Once they got started they could never stop
Singing, do you want a man of steel, or
Do you want a man that's real?
Some of them hide when the doorbell rings
They're only made of steel
    when they're on steel strings

Playing the man on steel strings
Playing the man on steel strings
Playing the man on steel strings
Playing the man on steel strings

Were you expecting maybe superman?
The best they do is the best they can
The manager's doing time in jail
The pink cadillac is up for sale
Singing, do you want a man of steel, or
Do you want a man that's real?
They'll try their hands at a thousand things
But they're only made of steel
    when they're on steel strings

Playing the man on steel strings
Playing the man on steel strings
Playing the man on steel strings
Playing the man on steel strings

Peter Case, 1986

Entella Hotel

There was no way of telling on the first day in town
How far it was from the Greyhound station to midnight,
　　and always
You checked into a room at the Entella Hotel
Got used to the gloom and the smell
And the thrill at the sight of old men laying in hallways

So you go up on Broadway where the sailors all roll
And the girls give themselves names like Lola, Estelle,
　　and Nicole
They work at a place called the Garden of Earthly Delights
And the tourists pour in from all over to take in the sights

In the sweet summer heat, Nick the Cop walks the beat
You feel him coming from way down the street
Drawing lines in the dirt at his feet and daring kids to cross it
Now all the same winos I still see in my dreams
Tighten up and start making scenes
And here comes Nick, all a-swagger
And the old ones are whispering, "Toss it!"
So Nick picks it up and looks for who's needing it most
And the ones on the lam are all getting ready to roast

And the afternoon goes on forever like some drunken bum
'Til the sun finally drowns 'neath the bridge and the night
　　has begun
Down by the bay, the ship's horns are blasting the fog
As we stumble and mutter and run through the gutter
　　like dogs
With one card to play and dyin' to play it each night
In the back of a bar called the Garden of Earthly Delights

Now, high in your room, the mirror falls with a roar
You're starin' in pieces that lay broke on the floor
And there's a knock on the door and the guy says there's a
　　call on the phone

You figure nobody knows your room or your name
You guess it's someone just playing a game
So you answer it guarded, expecting to still be alone
It's Nicole, she says she's gettin' off early tonight
Her and the boss just had a terrible fight
And would you come down to meet her, would that
    be alright?

So you walk in the back door and the first thing you hear
    is her song
At the Garden of Earthly Delights the show must go on
You got one card to play and you're dyin' to play it each
    night
In the back of the place called the Garden of Earthly
    Delights
You got one card to play and you're dyin' to play it
    tonight
With your back to the bar at the Garden of Earthly
    Delights

The Man with the Blue, Post-Modern, Fragmented,
Neo-Traditionalist, Guitar, 1989

Old Part of Town

Last night I wandered punch drunk and enraptured
Out on the beltway where the business is done
As I lay on the asphalt 'neath the glow of light boxes
I heard somebody say, "Bet I know where he's from"

When the town is so quiet you hear the bell tower tickin'
Out on the beltway they're still sellin' the chicken
Where the tempers are short and the hours are long
Darlin', won't you meet me in the old part of town?

Old part of town
You can still hear the footsteps of the old mystery
Old part of town
You can still feel the heartbeat of our whole history
When the heat on the street is wearin' you down
Darlin', won't you meet me in the old part of town?

Two red high heel shoes split up around midnight
They said they'd meet later by the fountain on Third
Four tires came screeching from different directions
And picked 'em both up 'fore they stepped off the curb

'Cause in the hours past midnight they stop keeping tabs
The carnival quarters are vacant and sad
But darlin' I think there's still a time to be had
In the old part of town where your mom met your dad
Darlin' won't you meet me in the old part of town?
Darlin' won't you meet me in the old part of town?

Old part of town
You can still hear the footsteps of the old mystery
Old part of town
You can still feel the heartbeat of our whole history
When the heat on the street is wearin' you down
Darlin', won't you meet me in the old part of town?

Saw a newspaper with big headlines that seemed to stare
    right through ya
Jump off a boxcar and blow into town
Pick a fight with two beer cans and a torn candy wrapper
The broom sweeping in the alley swore she never heard a
    sound

Meanwhile back on the beltway cars are waiting in lines
Stars are blocked out by the shine of the signs
You might want to say it's a sign of the times
But darlin' won't you meet me in the old part of town
Darlin' won't you meet me in the old part of town

Old part of town
You can still hear the footsteps of the old mystery
Old part of town
You can still feel the heartbeat of our whole history
When the heat on the street is wearin' you down
Darlin', won't you meet me in the old part of town?

The Man with the Blue, Post-Modern, Fragmented,
Neo-Traditionalist Guitar, 1989

Hidden Love

Far from the dreams, the bright lights and the boulevards
In these empty rooms a guitar makes a band
Our last conversation still echoes on bare walls
Like a child's painting of everything we planned

Across the brown fields and through the frozen meadows
All around this place we call our own
We all have to live here in each other's shadows
Hoping someday soon we'll be home

We kept a secret hidden deep inside
Hidden love, unbidden love
And all the tears we cried
Though I've loved you for a long time
Now it can't be denied
Someone sees the dreams we hide
Someone sees the dreams we hide
The dreams we hide

I woke up in the dark, stranded on the floor
Stripped of all my dreams and my pride
The vast black night that conquered me
    was coming back for more
When I turned and found the angel by my side

We kept a secret hidden deep inside
Hidden love, unbidden love
And all the tears we cried
Though I've loved you for a long time
Now it can't be denied
Someone sees the dreams we hide
Someone sees the dreams we hide
The dreams we hide

The Man with the Blue, Post-Modern, Fragmented,
Neo-Traditionalist Guitar, 1989

Poor Old Tom

A Tennessee boy joined the US Navy
In nineteen-fifty he was seventeen
A quiet kid who'd never seen the ocean
His mama died his first trip at sea

He learned to work and he learned to whistle
He learned to gamble and he learned to fight
He learned to suck a bottle and go out whorin'
Somehow he learned to stagger in at night

Poor old Tom, he don't know
Why his teeth gotta rattle, shiver and shake
The night wind's free to blow wherever it pleases
Tom's free to walk 'til the cold day break

Poor old Tom, he's telling it all
His thoughts are roaring like a waterfall
He never cared about money and there's no doubt
He never had much money to care about

Typhoons and calms on the great Pacific
Proud to be serving the USA
He worked hard on board and he got promoted
He got VD but it went away

Poor old Tom, he ain't right
He went out in San Francisco on a Saturday night
Sunday morning his ship set sail
Tom was resting in the Oakland jail

Now it's thirty-five years since his incarceration
On a morals charge—the words he said to me
From the brig on Treasure Island to the institution
They treated his depression with shock therapy

Poor old Tom, he don't know
He's got trouble recallin' his history
At the drop of a coin he'll start to ramble
How the whole damn thing's a mystery

His eyes bulge out as we talk on the corner
Eight turns on the gurney they held him down
One morning they wheeled him to another building
A surgery room with doctors standing 'round

He cried, "Lord help me," as they put him under
He sailed away on an ether sea
Ever since that day all he does is wonder
Did the surgeons perform a lobotomy?

Poor old Tom, this story's true
He's got nothin' to show, no one to show it to
The word for him is nevertheless
He fought for freedom, never took a free breath

Now the radios blare Nusak and Musak
Diseases are cured every day
The worst disease in the world is to be unwanted
To be used up and cast away

So as we make our way towards our destinations
Fortunes are still made with flesh and blood
Progress and love got nothing in common
Jesus healed a blind man's eyes with mud

Poor old Tom, he don't know
Why his teeth gotta rattle, shiver and shake
The night wind's free to blow wherever it pleases
Tom's free to walk 'til the cold day break

The Man with the Blue, Post-Modern, Fragmented,
Neo-Traditionalist Guitar, 1989

Put Down the Gun

On the hills outside of town there's a hiding place
Where the green fields sway with lavender, mustard and
    Queen Anne's Lace
Where the silent clouds go sailing in a sea of Dutchman's
    blue
And the lonesome tracks by the railroad cut make me think of
    you and a train we missed

I loved you from the first time I looked upon your face
Tho' I didn't know your story I could feel your wild grace
Now you got yourself in trouble, well, that ain't nothin'
    new
Through thick and thin there's always been someone
    watching over you

But you can put down your gun
Put down your gun
You can put down your gun
Put down your gun

So you grew up on a street where the cops don't go alone
In a town just like a wishing well you were cast in like a
    stone

But you can put down your gun
Put down your gun
Put down the gun and we'll talk

Your friends all throw their lives away just making the
    rounds
And they can't tell the difference between the shepherds
    and the clowns
Who go knocking down doors by the roadside everyday
Selling something you don't want at a price you don't
    have to pay

But you can put down your gun
Put down your gun
You can put down your gun
Put down your gun

It's a lonely road you've travelled that's led you to this wall
A road that's come unravelled like it ain't no road at all

But you can put down your gun
Put down your gun
You can put down the gun and we'll talk

Now I don't want to swear it but it's something that I heard
The gun in the first act always goes off in the third
I don't want to hurt you and I don't want to fight
But there'll be no third act at all if someone's killed tonight

You can put down your gun
Put down your gun
You can put down your gun
Put down your gun
Put down the gun and we'll talk

The Man with the Blue, Post-Modern, Fragmented,
Neo-Traditionalist Guitar, 1989

This Town's a Riot

I was standing on the corner of walk and don't walk
Trying to read the Spanish on the wall
It takes 15,000 pounds of pressure
Just to stand on that corner doing nothing at all

I was feeling just as broke as the ten commandments
When the earth started shaking like wash on a line
Everything went wrong and it felt like Christmas
When the power fails the poor will shine

C'mon darlin', let's go down
I'm all shook up and I can't sit down
I can't read and I can't write
But this town's a riot on a Saturday night
This town's a riot
This town's a riot
This town

There's people sick with hunger on the corner of
    Hope Street
Near a store selling x-rated wedding cake
The pope drove by and the bums got the bum's rush
Coyotes chased a horseback man in the lake

This town ain't no cheap hotel
There's no room to live or let
This town's a riot it's a jumble
It's a ride on a mumbo jumbo jet
This town's a riot
This town

Amazed by what you see on Main Street
Linin' up for the goof de jour
This town's a riot, it's a jungle
From the jailhouse steps to your own front door

In a room with a view of channel two
Wondering how much the lottery pays
Watch the miracle workers cleaning up the wreckage
Like you're waiting on a month of judgement days

C'mon darlin', let's go down
I'm all shook up and I can't sit down
I can't read and I can't write
But this towns' a riot on a Saturday night
This town's a riot
This town's a riot
This town

The Man with the Blue, Post-Modern, Fragmented,
Neo-Traditionalist Guitar, 1989

Travelin' Light

You've been standin' on the corner for a thousand nights
It's the slowest corner known to man
Watchin' strange faces passin' 'neath the lights
With a bottle wavin' in your hand

You got just enough money for some nothin' to go
It ain't exactly what you planned
So lonesome that you can't even say hello
And no one seems to understand

So you're a mixed up kid, come on and join the crowd
Of the ones that only fit where they're not allowed
Out on the streets and you're feelin' blue
Travelin' light
You got a hole in your soul where the wind blows through
A hole in your soul where the wind blows through

You wandered away from your childhood home
No one cared to trace the tracks you laid
You traveled by night and you traveled alone
Came to rest at a penny arcade

Well the last shots over on a Saturday night
You wake up in the beam of a cop's flashlight
He asks you who you are as if you knew or you cared
He's askin' where you live and you just say nowhere

So you're a mixed up kid, come on and join the crowd
Of the ones that only fit where they're not allowed
Out on the streets and you're feelin' blue
Travelin' light
You got a hole in your soul where the wind blows through
A hole in your soul where the wind blows through

Travelin' light all your big mistakes
And the trouble that you found could be your saving grace
A prayer of a chance out of the blue
Asking for a miracle to see you through

Well, I don't know where I got it but I got it the same
It's a feelin' that'll rip me apart
It follows me around like a part of my name
Like I'm born with a time bomb instead of a heart

So I'm mixed up, kid, come on and join the crowd
Of the ones that only fit where they're not allowed
Out on the streets and I'm feelin' blue
Travelin' light
With a hole in my soul where the wind blows through
A hole in my soul where the wind blows through

(Peter Case, Bob Neuwirth)

The Man with the Blue, Post-Modern, Fragmented,
Neo-Traditionalist Guitar, 1989

Two Angels

That must have been two angels
Or was it you and me?
That must have been two angels
Or was it you and me?
Now those angels have flown
And left us here on our own, how can it be?

We fell in love on the night we met
We fell in love on the night we met
How those angels of love came down from above
I can't forget

That must have been two angels
Or was it you and me?
That must have been two angels
Was it you and me?
Now those angels have flown
They left us here on our own—how can it be?

The wind through the leaves
    was a whisper and sigh
Oh, the wind through the leaves
    was a whisper and sigh
All the stars in the night were angels of light
For you and I

That must have been two angels or was it you and me?
That must have been two angels was it you and me?
Now those angels have flown
And left us here on our own—how can it be?

Now those angels have gone
Left us here to carry on—how can it be?

That must have been two angels
That must have been two angels
That must have been two angels
That must have been two angels

The Man with the Blue, Post-Modern, Fragmented,
Neo-Traditionalist Guitar, 1989

Beyond the Blues

The old man on the corner is singing my life
He's playing guitar with a rusty old knife
Each line that he sings rhymes with the truth
And promise of something beyond the blues
Beyond the blues

You and me, darling, took the long way around
'Cross the wide open country
    past the heart attack towns
We hit the fork in the road
    where we all have to choose
Between darkness and life beyond the blues
Beyond the blues

Beyond the shadows, beyond the rain
Beyond the trouble, beyond the pain
When you know in your heart there's no way out
    but through
Take a walk with me, darlin', beyond the blues
Beyond the blues

The old man on the corner has been gone for years
His guitar and the knife are all rusty with tears
But there's a song that he gave us we never have to lose
About another life waiting beyond the blues
Beyond the blues

Beyond the shadows, beyond the rain
Beyond the trouble, beyond the pain
When you know in your heart there's no way out
    but through
Take a walk with me, darlin', beyond the blues
Beyond the blues

Love is the road beyond the blues

(Peter Case, Bob Neuwirth, Tom Russell)

Six Pack Of Love, 1992

Dream About You

At the cellar door
    I dream about you
With the grain on the floor
    I dream about you

A five alarm fool
    fresh out of time
    then you come along
Turn the dime store
    into a diamond mine

I dream about you
I can't help myself
I dream about you

You're never far away
    from me somehow
All I do is call your name
    I see you so clearly now

I dream about you
    and then I wake up
The dreams disappear
    over my coffee cup

Shut down for good
    the day of the crime
I misunderstood
Then I see your eyes
    in the back of my mind

You're the living proof
    I dream about you
I watch from the roof
    I dream about you

(Peter Case, Andrew Williams)

Six Pack Of Love, 1992

Airplane

Outside the colosseum we stole the flying machine
With your arms wrapped around my waist you took a
    ride with me
Over lakes and rich green forests, way out in the wild
'Til we ran out of gas and crashed after one last magic mile

Won't you let me ride on your airplane?
I've been living on a landing strip watching your runway
Everything in the whole wide world could flow so easily
If you'd only come down and fly
Take an airplane ride with me

We came down through the treetops and hit the ground
    so hard
I came to by a picket fence in an elderly couple's yard
That's when you turned into a man and wanted to go back
'Til we saw the houndstooth interior and stole their
    Cadillac

Won't you let me ride on your airplane?
I've been living on a landing strip watching your runway
Everything in the whole wide world could flow so easily
If you'd only come down and fly
Take an airplane ride with me

The policeman pulled us over and started to run a make
Stealing that El Dorado was looking like a big mistake
He threatened jail, named the bail, I was broke but on a roll
On a corner of the highway I'd never seen before

Won't you let me ride on your airplane?
I've been living on a landing strip watching your runway
Everything in the whole wide world could flow so easily
If you'd only come down and fly
Take an airplane ride with me

Torn Again, 1995

Blind Luck

Here comes Blind Luck swingin' his cane
I wonder what he's gonna try and pull today
He's always got a few tricks up his sleeve
I've seen him play a few tricks you wouldn't believe

Here comes Blind Luck calling your name
He's got a new set of rules to a brand new game
He's gonna make an offer that you can't refuse
He has a way of knowing who's got something to lose

You can hedge your bets, or you can play the odds
Deal with the devil, or go with God
It's anybody's game when the wheel starts to spin
Somebody's gonna lose, somebody else win

Now here comes Blind Luck, he's your long lost friend
When the stakes are right he's always back again
Tappin' on your shoulder while you wait your turn
Standin' in your corner when there's money to burn

So you bet it all on the black thirteen
Then you close your eyes and start to dream
Of a brand new chance in a bar uptown
Then your hands start shakin' as the wheel slows down

So here comes Blind Luck in his new pair of shades
A pocketful of money somebody else made
A new white suit and a French silk tie
He's crossin' against the traffic with his head held high

And all the evidence points to providence
But your common sense says coincidence
So when the deal goes down
For the lost and found
Whether you win or lose
You got the Blind Luck blues

(Peter Case, Fred Koller)

Torn Again, 1995

The Wilderness

We were marching down the Orange Plank Road
When the federals first we spied
By the old Wilderness Tavern
The armies did collide

Lead began to fill
And whistle through the air
The dead and dying piled up
Their blood was everywhere

In the Wilderness
I was just seventeen
By far the bloody angle
Was the worst I'd ever seen
In the Wilderness

We broke in disorder
And fled into the pines
Tangled in the underbrush
We couldn't find our lines

We faced 'em there for hours
'Til it grew too dark to fight
And the moans and cries for water
Went unanswered in the night

In the Wilderness
All the early days of June
Lying with the dying
'Neath the green Virginia moon

In the Wilderness
Where the Devil tempted Christ
Lee got on the radio
And ordered up a strike
In the Wilderness

So we set the woods on fire
And stopped 'em in their tracks
We laughed as we saw 'em running
And shot 'em in their backs
They never saw it coming
From the guns up in the trees
So we let 'em have it one more time
As they fell down to their knees
In the Wilderness

I was way out in the Wilderness
With the Stonewall Brigade
The Captain saw my wound and said, "Son
Praying ain't my trade"

The jets went roaring over
We beheld the pride of Mars
With hearts the size of houses
And eyes that blazed like stars

In the Wilderness
Where the serpent wears a crown
There were angels in the treetops
As I lay my body down

In the Wilderness
I was just seventeen
By far the bloody angle
Was the worst I'd ever see
In the Wilderness

Torn Again, 1995

Turning Blue

He tugs at the tie, shrugs off the jacket
Lays his head down on the floral design
A whiff of cologne, the little dab that did ya'
His watch on the end table keeps perfect time
Yeah, his watch on the end table keeps perfect time

By a second floor window and a half lowered shade
She stands by the sash rubbing her jaw
Goose bumps in down, white scars on her forearms
The floorboards are drying as the afternoon fades

Turning blue
The whole wide world is turning blue
Turning blue
Deep watered down celestial blue
Deep watered down dirty celestial blue

She's watching tail lights as the snowflakes are swirling
Man on the sofa stirring lightly at first
She lights a smoke at the stove and then turning
Flicks a short ash towards his clothes by her purse

Turning blue
The whole wide world is turning blue
Turning blue
Deep watered down celestial blue
Deep watered down dirty celestial blue

Now there's a crash in the hallway, loud feet on the stairs
Someone's pounding the door trying to break it in two
Man on the sofa rises cartoonish
His face out of focus as it comes into view

Knocked off and shattered she flies to the window
Reaching for something and coming up air
Who's at the door, have they come here to kill us?
Have they come here to save us or just to kill you?

If I could go home I'd leave in the morning
I'd ride on the Greyhound if it's all I could do
Go back to my mother the people I come from
Hide 'neath the sheets as the world's turning blue

Turning blue
The whole wide world is turning blue
Turning blue
Deep watered down blue
Deep watered down dirty celestial blue

Torn Again, 1995

A Little Wind (Could Blow Me Away)

The little girl had a hound dog
Hound dog tree'd a 'coon
'Coon stirred up a hornet's nest
That swarmed up to the moon
A little wind could blow me away

The moon he started laughing
Fell into the lake
Black water boiled and bubbled
The earth began to shake
A little wind could blow me away

Trip me up on a grain of sand
Drown me in a drop of rain
One tiny spark and I go right up in flames
A little wind could blow me away
A little wind could blow me away

Earth kept right on shaking
The little wind was just a breeze
It was raining alligators
Black snakes fell from trees
A little wind could blow me away

The little girl and the hound dog
They were trying to make it home
Through the snakes and alligators
They were hopping stone to stone
A little wind could blow me away

Trip me up on a grain of sand
Drown me in a drop of rain
One tiny spark and I go right up in flames
A little wind could blow me away
A little wind could blow me away

The stones kept right on rolling
Sky was turning red
The little wind reached out a hand
And carried her home to bed
A little wind could blow me away

She could hear the freight train wailing
Rain crows came awake
She could hear her hound dog bayin'
As the day began to break
A little wind could blow me away

Trip me up on a grain of sand
Drown me in a drop of rain
One tiny spark and I go right up in flames
A little wind could blow me away
A little wind could blow me away

(Peter Case, Tom Russell)

Torn Again, 1995

Crooked Mile

I left my mother's house at fifteen, with a dime and
    a suit of clothes
All set to hitch the first car by and ride to where it goes
But who's gonna go your crooked mile?

I got to New York City where they looked me up
    and down
At knife point off St. Mark's Place I gave up the crown
Who's gonna go your crooked mile?

Who's gonna go your crooked mile?
Who's gonna haul your load?
Who's gonna come out in the dark and find you on
    that road?
Who's gonna go your crooked mile?
Who's gonna go your crooked mile?

Out in California I was spinning 'neath blue skies
When I fell hard all for a girl with rain drops in her eyes
Who's gonna go your crooked mile?

Who's gonna hold your lily-white hand, who's gonna
    drive you south?
Who's gonna be your morning dove, kiss you on the
    mouth?
Who's gonna go your crooked mile?

Who's gonna go your crooked mile?
Who's gonna haul your load?
Who's gonna come out in the dark to find you on
    that road?

So when my run was over I fell down on my knees
And I felt the touch of the Holy Ghost when I said,
    "Jesus, please"
Who's gonna go your crooked mile?

Well, my way sure runs crooked, the highway's up above
The only thing I found that counts in this world is love
Who's gonna go your crooked mile?

Who's gonna go your crooked mile?
Who's gonna haul your load?
Who's gonna come out in the dark and find you on
    your road?
Who's gonna go your crooked mile?
Who's gonna go your crooked mile?
Who's gonna go your crooked mile?
Tell me who is gonna go your crooked mile?

Full Service No Waiting, 1997

On the Way Downtown

How many times have I washed my face
Combed my hair and left this place?
Felt the shiver in my chest when I hit the door
The promise of something here worth living for

Had a fight with the woman that had my kids
Can't get along with anyone, what if I did?
I'm going back to the corner where we used to meet
When our dreams were young and the nights were sweet

I'm going out tonight going way downtown
Where my friends who died still hang around
See what's shaking as the leaves turn brown
The season's been and gone
But there's another one coming on
And I'm on my way downtown

Thirty years ago in the setting sun
I was walking down Union and I started to run
Down into a cellar where the music screamed
I guess it hit me harder than I ever dreamed

At the Palace Theater later on that night
There were miracles in store but not a soul in sight
Payphone ringing didn't seem so strange
Anything could happen, everything could change

I'm going out tonight, way downtown
Where my friends hang around
All that moonlight spilling on the ground
The season's been and gone
But there's another one coming on
And I'm on my way downtown

We used to gather here flirt and laugh
Now all my dreams are cut in half
The girls are smoking cigarettes and chewing gum
They just get scared when they see me come

Way downtown the corner's moved
The sandstone slabs are worn and grooved
Turning black in the first drops of rain
You can smell the earth and sky again

Hear the rattle of the leaves, the locust's call
Underneath the elms by the schoolyard wall
Summer's over and the fields are tall
The season's been and gone
But there's another one coming on
And I'm on my way downtown

(Peter Case, Joshua Case)

Full Service, No Waiting, 1997

Spell of Wheels

Kansas City as the first snow of the year begins to fall
She's at a Westport party drunk and leaning against
    the wall
Skip and Wolf come stomping in, someone has a plan
Faceboy goes to fetch his clothes, I go to lend a hand

We leave KC at midnight heading north on the interstate
Snow is falling hard and fast, we're glad to get away
Five kids in a beat up car kickin' up their heels
Heading out into the dark beneath the spell of wheels
Beneath the spell of wheels

Across the land this car will roll
Past places we'll never know
Flashing lights and highway signs
Mark the miles and keep the time
Beneath the spell of wheels
Beneath the spell of wheels

It's an empty stretch of pitch black road
And we're feeling quite upset
The snow is falling harder now
We're scared as we can get
'Cause the black car that's been chasing us
Has rolled its window down
And when I see the shotgun there
I know we're graveyard bound

High above us in the night
A thousand faces sleep in flight
Down here the road turns like a screw
I'm on my way back home to you
Beneath the spell of wheels
Beneath the spell of wheels

Now we're sinkin' low as we can go
And waitin' for the blast
Skippie jams down on the brakes
That demon car blows past
We pull off on the roadside
Everybody pulls their knives
The black car keeps on goin'
And I guess so do our lives

We get to Minnesota
Spend the winter in monochrome
Fall in with small time criminals
Just like the ones at home
Watchin' through the windows
For what the night reveals
Waitin' for the spring to come
Beneath the spell of wheels
Beneath the spell of wheels

(Peter Case, Joshua Case)

Full Service, No Waiting, 1997

Blue Distance

Up on Black Mountain we stood on the ledge
With our backs to the stone and our feet on the edge
To watch the world spin, clouds gathering
And to wonder what the years and miles would bring

In the blue distance with you
Just for a moment I nearly broke through
Into the blue distance with you

Summer passed quickly, under a spell
What seemed like forever, it's a story to tell
Darkness is falling, storms moving in
And there ain't no telling if we'll be here again

In the blue distance with you
Just for a moment I nearly broke through
Into the blue distance with you

There's no moon tonight, as to whether we start
Depends on how well you can see with your heart
I've lost my direction, I've looked up and down
I can't find the connection when you're not around

In the blue distance with you
Just for a moment I nearly broke through
Into the blue distance with you

Up on Black Mountain I'm not afraid
Of a place where I'm free or a price to be paid
But I've never known any better than this
Except for one morning's sweet promise of bliss

In the blue distance with you
Just for a moment I nearly broke through
Into the blue distance with you

In the blue distance with you
Just for a moment I nearly broke through
Into the blue distance with you

Flying Saucer Blues, 2000

Cold Trail Blues

Cold trail blues
I could use
Any kind of sign
That you're still on the line

Cold trail blues
I've been searching round the world for you
No matter how I call
I'm no closer at all

It's almost like you never came
I swear I almost lost your name
Once you meant so much to me
I thought your love would set me free

Cold trail blues
Something I need that I just can't find
Is it too late now?
Am I too far behind?

Well, there's a whole new crowd out there
And they just don't seem to care
Still I keep searching in this gloom
I'll find your trail right through this room

Cold trail blues
Something I need that I just can't see
Is it too late now?
You're inside of me

Cold trail blues
I could use
Any kind of sign
That you're still on the line

Any kind of sign
You're still on the line
Cold trail blues
Cold trail blues
Cold trail blues

Flying Saucer Blues, 2000

Paradise, Etc.

The road I've been on since I was two
Well I just found out that it don't go through

Payday passed, my ship came and went
The apocalypse is over and I still owe rent

They say love is learned when the heart turns stone
Prayer begins when you can't go on

My heart's been rocked, the road is blocked
Is that rain I hear, drip drop drip drop?

I'm bound for cloudland, dreamland, fairyland
Canaan, Goshen, Shangri-la
Elysium, Arcadia
Paradise, etcetera

She says so what and I don't care
Laughs at the mention of underwear
Gets mad and pouts when it's time to eat
I'm afraid she'll run out in the street

I'm in charge but I get there late
I may be large but I hesitate
Everything's gonna work out fine
When we get across that borderline

We'll be in cloudland, dreamland, fairyland
Canaan, Goshen, Shangri-la
Elysium, Arcadia
Paradise, etcetera

The blue serene, the hyaline
Seventh heaven on cloud nine
The realm of light, the world above
Milk and honey and a snow white dove

The land of bliss and la ti da
Paradise, etcetera

The got-rocks are home in bed
Newlyweds and nearly deads
But we're stuck in this primordial ooze
With a case of flying saucer blues

Now this might be our last broadcast
If we don't think of something fast
Someday I'll sing and the songs will come
To lift the hearts of everyone

Down here in cloudland, dreamland, fairyland
Canaan, Goshen, Shangri-la
Elysium, Arcadia
Paradise, etcetera

additional lyrics:

From Beulah Land to Jerusalem
Eden's hand to Kingdom Come
The ancient source of Cibola
A date with the queen of Mardi Gras

Flying Saucer Blues, 2000

Two Heroes

In a five story walk-up, Hollywood dump
Lived a fighter from Kentucky
    who couldn't take a punch
Albert Jackson's his name—from Louisville
With his lady Francine who was paying the bills

He got out of the fight game
    while he still had his wits
Nobody noticed when he called it quits
Nights Albert walked to the corner for beer
An eight battery box blasting loud in his ear

Two heroes are better than one
What justice under the sun?
One with a Bible, one with a gun
These days two heroes are better than one

Two teenage girls lived a couple floors down
Roomin' with a stranger who just got to town
One night about eight the gals walked out the door
And a carload of toughs thought they'd just found a score

They pulled alongside—a guy jumped out with a knife
Said, "give me your money or you'll pay with your life"
The girls were so frightened they couldn't move
Time stopped dead, no one knew what to do

Two heroes are better than one
What justice under the sun?
One with a Bible, one with a gun
These days two heroes are better than one

No one saw Albert coming back from the store
He took a quick look didn't need to see more
He lifted his box cracked that thief on the head
Who sank to the pavement with his hair turning red

Oh yeah! Oh yeah? Yeah.

Albert beats it inside after giving the hit
The carload of guys grab their friend and then split
But not before the stranger who blew into town
Comes out waving a pistol and fires a round

Everybody vanishes like alakazam
When the cops show up they're happy as clams
Shots are reported, there's blood on the ground
Someone dropped a dime and now there's no one around

Two heroes are better than one
What justice under the sun?
You might think it's over but it's hardly begun
These days two heroes are better than one

The paddy wagon comes and they fill it like this
A guy in pajamas takes his dog for piss
He's first to go but hold the cigar
Here comes a neighbor out moving his car

Pretty soon suspects three, four, five and six
Are all wearing cuffs and taking their licks
An anonymous source says now they know the one
"It's the black dude on the fifth floor who fired the gun!"

Now the SWAT team arrives and they start to climb
Taking the stars three at a time
Up to the fifth floor where I hear this sound:
"ALBERT OPEN THE DOOR OR WE'RE KNOCKING
    IT DOWN!"

Now Albert's inside and he's all in a rush
To get his pot from the planter to the bowl for a flush
They kick down his door, put his head in a lock
And choke hold drag him to the lobby knock knock

Oh yeah! Oh yeah? Yeah.

And just as they're about to pull away for the jail
Here comes the pale stranger with the girls on his tail
He confesses, "It was me—I fired the shots
These are my girls—I'm just protecting the tots"

"I'm here from Arizona—hiding out—on the lam
On the run—a convict—escaped from the slam
I feel bad for these people—you might think I'm nuts—
It should be me in those chains—
   I know it down in my guts"

Two heroes are better than one
What justice under the sun?
One with a Bible, one with a gun
These days two heroes are better than one

So later on that same night the cops let everyone go
Except for of course the stars of the show
Turns out the stranger robbed a bank
   to finance his flight
And the charges 'gainst Albert
   well they didn't sound right

Now the stranger's doin' twenty in his previous home
The girls are both models and they're living in Rome
Last I saw Albert he and Francine were down
Nursing their bruises and suing the town

Two heroes are better than one
What justice under the sun?
One with a Bible, one with a gun
These days two heroes are better than one

(Peter Case, LeRoy Marinell)

Flying Saucer Blues, 2000

Gone

I thought I'd escape to San Francisco
I was on the run from everything
Slipping round the corners, dodging out back doors
No care or thought to what the nights would bring

Gone, gone, everything is gone
And I don't know what to do
Gone, gone, everything is gone
Still I keep wondering 'bout you

I got to California in the springtime
Saw you there when I stepped off the train
Time passes slow—was that a hundred years ago?
We were walking by the Mission in the rain

Gone, gone, everything is gone
And I don't know what to do
Gone, gone, everything is gone
Still I keep wondering 'bout you

"I get the feeling your luck's going to change
Now the road is clear, the sky is blue
Here comes your someday for turning the page
May you find the one who can make it all come true"

Summer 'round the hills of San Francisco
Gone again and I just got the news
Propped up on the strand, with my head in my hands
Coin toss on Grant Ave with the blues

Gone, gone, everything is gone
And I don't know what to do
Gone, gone, everything is gone
Still I keep wondering 'bout you

"I get the feeling your luck's going to change
Now the road is clear, the sky is blue
Here comes your someday for turning the page
May you find the one who can make it all come true"

Beeline, 2002

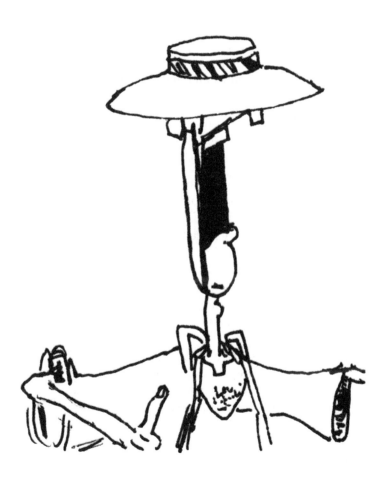

I Hear Your Voice

Down your street we come humming, swinging a tune
Returning to your place in the late afternoon
Sun flowing gold, sky blue and cool
Breathless and bold like two kids outta school

I hear your voice
Everywhere I go

Climbing the stairs up to your floor
A kiss in the hallway unlocking the door
Dreams coming true and it's about time
As the light starts falling and the mission bells chime

I hear your voice
Everywhere I go
Everywhere I go

We stood there in front of the club on your street
Just separated by a couple of feet
So glad to be living, this moment to see
In the glow of your presence I'm finally free

The city surrounds us with five kinds of light
Neon and sunset, the traffic at night
The look in your eyes, the ring of your talk
The sparks from the ashes and your heels on the walk

Magic returned on the N Judah line
'Neath the radio tower and the power light's shine
On the J by the stairs, 'neath the trees in the park
By the corner and leaning 'gainst walls in the dark

I hear your voice
Everywhere I go
Everywhere I go

You only live once or twice I heard you say
I hear you speaking when I'm faraway
Well, I'm goin' out for a minute or two
And when I get back I'll be looking for you

I hear your voice
Everywhere I go
Everywhere I go
Everywhere I go
Everywhere I go

Beeline, 2002

Kokomo Prayer Vigil

The loneliest road in America
Is twenty-thousand miles all the way around
Don't get lost runnin' east of St Louis
There ain't no money if this thing breaks down

America comes in two great flavors
Of angry voices on the radio
"This is Preacher Bob calling on election eve
For a prayer night vigil in Kokomo"

So I drove that car 'til my back wore out
'Til I was talking to myself making animal sounds
Growling, howling, crying blind
And rubbing hands over my face and crown

Pulled into a truck stop jammed with cars
Hot nuts, coffee and gasoline
Lined up for kingsize candy bars
Red Bull four-pack hick routines

America comes in two great flavors
Of angry voices on the radio
"This is Preacher Bob calling on election eve
For a prayer night vigil in Kokomo"

East of El Paso near the border
A sudden checkpoint's stoppin' cars
A lonesome machine gun jack boot soldier
Points the weapon and his eyes meet mine

A misunderstanding—I keep driving
He gets excited and starts to shout
"What's your hurry!" then he aims the barrel
At my head and waves me out

America is on the move
Red Sox on the radio
Static from the glowing dial
Fading in and out with Preacher Joe

I hitched out of D.C. one early spring
To New York City with a couple of friends
1970 Vietnam March
Half a million strong faced the president

And the army was on the treasury roof
Machine guns trained on the mighty crowd
I was fifteen and the world seemed wide
Compared to what I see here now

America comes in two great flavors
Of angry voices on the radio
"This is Preacher Bob calling on election eve
For a prayer night vigil in Kokomo"

Bomblight Prayer Vigil, 2006

Ain't Gonna Worry No More

Bare feet poppin' on a pinewood floor
A tumble rush of desert flowers 'side the door
Her music box is pretty with the piebald stripes
Dust mote diamonds in a shaft of light

C'mon down, I ain't gonna worry no more
C'mon down, I ain't gonna worry no more
Everybody's laughin', now it won't be long
We've seen a lot of trouble, now the ghost is gone
C'mon down, I ain't gonna worry no more
I ain't gonna worry no more

Waiting at the depot for a London train
Trying to paint a picture in the pourin' rain
Hanging out a window, runnin' out of blue
Tomcat in the alley dodged a worn out shoe

C'mon down, I ain't gonna worry no more
C'mon down, I ain't gonna worry no more
Everybody's laughin', now it won't be long
We've seen a lot of trouble, now the ghost is gone
C'mon down, I ain't gonna worry no more
I ain't gonna worry no more

Open farmhouse window with a cooling pie
Fanned out on the breeze aroma called me nigh
I grabbed the dish and runnin' kept the right hand road
Crossing open country with my shoulder bowed

C'mon down, I ain't gonna worry no more
C'mon down, I ain't gonna worry no more
Everybody's laughin', now it won't be long
We've seen a lot of trouble, now the ghost is gone
C'mon down, I ain't gonna worry no more
I ain't gonna worry no more

I can hardly remember, I can almost recall
The first gig we played at the old Moose hall
Larry on bass Lloyd on tubs
Down in the catacombs before we ever took drugs

C'mon down, I ain't gonna worry no more
C'mon down, I ain't gonna worry no more
Everybody's laughin', now it won't be long
We've seen a lot of trouble, now the ghost is gone
C'mon down, I ain't gonna worry no more
I ain't gonna worry no more

He's fourteen dressed in his father's hat
Even grew a little mustache just like that
Told the crazy lady at the corner shop
"I'll take a pack of Camels and a bottle of schnapps"

C'mon down, I ain't gonna worry no more
C'mon down, I ain't gonna worry no more
Everybody's laughin', now it won't be long
We've seen a lot of trouble, now the ghost is gone
C'mon down, I ain't gonna worry no more
I ain't gonna worry no more

Back then they had a war that weren't no good
Everybody said they'd do what they could
Some went to Canada, some went down
With the FBI to the jail downtown

C'mon down, I ain't gonna worry no more

Bananas are cheap, that's United Fruit
They tore out the labor unions at the root
Murdered the tribes to clear the way
For the puppet government and CIA

C'mon down...

Hear the roar of jets coming over the park
The glow of last cigarettes in the dark
Do your bones turn to water? Does the sky turn black?
Ground zero in a missile attack

C'mon down, I ain't gonna worry no more

I was walking by a theater saw a shining sign
Said, "Lightnin' Hopkins playing here tonight"
Paid my last three bucks—went inside
And there he was in the big spotlight, singin'

C'mon down, I ain't gonna worry no more
C'mon down, I ain't gonna worry no more
Everybody's laughin', now it won't be long
We've seen a lot of trouble, now the ghost is gone
C'mon down, I ain't gonna worry no more
I ain't gonna worry no more

The sweetest woman that I've ever known
If I die tomorrow 'fore I turn to stone
I'll close my eyes, travel back in time
23rd and Mission, walking side by side

C'mon down, I ain't gonna worry no more
C'mon down, I ain't gonna worry no more
Everybody's laughing, now it won't be long
We've seen a lot of trouble, now the ghost is gone
C'mon down, I ain't gonna worry no more
I ain't gonna worry no more

Born beneath a wandering star
Never thought I'd get this far
I may be cracked but it's just as well
My ears are ringing like the Liberty Bell
C'mon down, I ain't gonna worry no more
C'mon down, I ain't gonna worry no more
Everybody's laughin', now it won't be long
We've seen a lot of trouble, now the ghost is gone
C'mon down, I ain't gonna worry no more
I ain't gonna worry no more
I ain't gonna worry no more
I ain't gonna worry no more

Let Us Now Praise Sleepy John, 2007

Every 24 Hours

Driving twelve hours after the show
Hit the border at dawn and kept going
As the moon crossed my path, I was doing the math
Will I make it? There's no way of knowing

I should've called home 'fore
    she went to sleep
Now I pray the lord for
    her soul to keep
Tomorrow will tell
    who's been tending the sheep
The world turns every twenty-four hours

Under a bridge in the black squalling rain
I could see then but just for an instant
As the wind hauled the morning off like a train
And the skyline was lost in the distance

Who moved the furniture?
Who hit the light?
Everything's changing
    but nothin' seems right
I thought I was smart
    but that was last night
The world turns every twenty-four hours

It turns every twenty-four hours
The world turns every twenty-four hours

The arrows were down and the road through the town
Was blocked by the flood and a crash site
The cop waved me through but I thought of you
'Cross ten thousand miles of moonlight

Life's opportunity
    moves with great speed
Pay close attention
    it's not guaranteed
We live in a whirl of
    wonder and greed
And it turns every twenty-four hours

It turns every twenty-four hours
The world turns every twenty-four hours
The world turns every twenty-four hours
The world turns every twenty-four hours

Let Us Now Praise Sleepy John, 2007

Somebrightmorningblues

The sky is clear, the air is cold
Rose lights shine, an asphalt road
It's been a while since I was born
Far from home I'm feeling worn
Alone forsaken—no that's yesterday
There's still 500 miles and a show to play

Sure, I've been through some dry long spells
Lonesome nights and prison cells
Mixed up summers made no sense
Dangling on a wooden fence
Worked so hard I guess I lost my place
My only wish tonight's to see your face

Some bright morning in the sun
I'll say goodbye to everyone
Some bright morning when this life is through
That's some bright morning
Some bright morning blues

Magic potions have a way
Of wearing off again someday
Celestial shores—who can believe?
If I did I'd never grieve
No need for worry if you know to pray
If I knew where to go I'd go today

Some bright morning in the sun
I'll say goodbye to everyone
Some bright morning when I've paid my dues
That's some bright morning
Some bright morning blues
That's some bright morning
Some bright morning blues

Let Us Now Praise Sleepy John, 2007

That Soul Twist

Another night, another show
Another day, so far to go
A couple hours, motel room
I'll be back on the highway soon

Forget tomorrow—the jam you're in
You're alive right now as you ever been
The line I shoot will never miss
That's the old soul twist

The judge ignored your earnest pleas
Truth was bought, lies were eased
Come on down, try to sleep
Rest your eyes, stay off your feet

You can walk the moon
Or swim the sea
If it's not too late it'll never be
Hold the treasure in your fist
Let it go—that's the old soul twist

Bang it, dang it
Hang it on the wall
Throw it out window
Run and catch it 'fore it falls
Used to go like that
Now it goes like this
Time to do that old soul twist

Pressure's on, money's tight
Everything will be alright
Stay awake, stay alert
Do the things you know will work

The only strength
Is the strength to live
The only life
Is the life we give
Live to give, that's the word
And all the wisdom that I've heard
Used to go like that
    and now it goes like this

That's the old soul twist
That old soul twist

Let Us Now Praise Sleepy John, 2007

The Open Road Song

On the raggly wooded outskirts of the city
Where the ancient elevators store the grain
And the long lake boats that used to haul the metal
Are in the dock and rusting with the rain

There's a maritime supply beneath the skyway
My father took me there to buy a rope
The store is dark and jammed with all you needed
For a journey 'round the Cape of Good Hope

I'll seek my fortune in the wide world
I'll take my chances in the cold
Come what may, I'll be OK
If I could only find a stretch of open road

A mysterious figure passes on the sidewalk
In ragged clothes, "Father," I say, "how come
He wears several dirty jackets and a topcoat?"
My father nods and says, "Son, that man's a bum"

I looked again and saw the rapt expression
'Neath the floppy hat he tipped back with his thumb
The aura of a world's ragtime adventure
I said, "When I grow up I want to be a bum"

I'll seek my fortune in the wide world
Take my chances in the cold
Come what may, I'll be OK
If I could only find a stretch of open road

Now, I'm traveling a world that's filled with war zones
Listening to music we've destroyed
Praying to a God who's just a tyrant
For work that's just like being unemployed

Eating food that's pumped with fat and water
Reading books with nothing on the page
Sitting in the dark to watch a picture
You're better hungry watching a bare stage

I'll seek my fortune in the wide world
Take my chances out there in the cold
Come what may, I'll be OK
If I could only find a stretch of open road

Let Us Now Praise Sleepy John, 2007

Underneath the Stars

It's cold outside, Lord help those
Lost tonight with the freezing toes
In the dark with the rain drenched clothes
She's all the way down

The sky has cleared, the stars are bright
The temperature's gonna fall tonight
In the park looking for a light
In a hospital gown

Underneath the stars
City by the sea
Headlights of the cars
Shine but no one sees
In another world
Just five feet away
Look into her eyes
"God bless" is all she'll say

Some drink wine, some are smokin' crack
This lady all alone wants none of that
In the park with a cart and sack
Afraid she's gonna drown

A choice she made not long ago
Has led to this, how could you know?
The door slammed shut, her children go
To whatever life they've found

Underneath the stars
City by the sea
Headlights of the cars
Shine but no one sees
In another world
Just five feet away

Look into her eyes
"God bless" is all she'll say

Now the clergy have their doubts
Are they helping lazy layabouts?
Late at night the drunken louts
Terrify the town

The cops are young, well they're just kids
They don't know about the skids
They just do what the gentry bids
From the other end of town

Underneath the stars
City by the sea
Headlights of the cars
Shine but no one sees
In another world
Just five feet away
Look into her eyes
"God bless" is all she'll say

Asleep in the park rain or shine
A thousand crows on a telephone line
Ask her how and she'll say fine
She's all the way down

Dew drops shot like cannonballs
Crash on paper prison walls
Her heart stops beating, the breathing stalls
She's dying all alone

Underneath the stars
City by the sea
Headlights of the cars
Shine but no one sees
In another world

Just five feet away
Look into her eyes
"God bless" is all she'll say

So now you ask what can I do?
See and know, they're just like you
You could wind up in the blue
Or beneath a pauper's crown

Don't be afraid, you'll be surprised
When you look into her eyes
You'll find a soulful feeling rise
You're all the way down

Underneath the stars
City by the sea
Headlights of the cars
Shine but no one sees
In another world
Just five feet away
Look into her eyes
"God bless" is all she'll say

Let Us Now Praise Sleepy John, 2007

A Million Dollars Bail

She dialed 911 but the cops didn't come on time
They found her on the marble with a bullet through
  her eye
He was weaving back and forth, foaming at the lips
So they took him in for questioning and inked his
  fingertips

There's two kinds of justice, everybody knows
One for folks up on the hill, the other's down below
Everyone is talking 'bout the night he spent in jail
Today he's free, out walking on a million dollars bail

They said she was a single girl that lived a double life
He'd met her at the hatcheck stand and took her home
  that night
No one knows what happened 'cuz no one else was there
No trial date was ever set and no one seems to care

There's two kinds of justice, everybody knows
One for folks up on the hill, the other's down below
Everyone is talking 'bout the night he spent in jail
Today he's free, out walking on a million dollars bail
On a million dollars bail

They tell us all the world is small and life is selling cheap
Anything can happen when you're walking in your sleep
The court took charge and eyed the facts, bail was set at
  one cool mil
Calls were made and debts were paid, the lawyers
  worked with skill

Eternity is longer than one night inside a box
And if you're heading for the jailhouse
Now's the time to pick the locks

There's a sentence passed on every soul, someday we
    all must die

When the question's not who pulls the switch, it's how
    you lived and why

There's two kinds of justice, everybody knows
One for folks up on the hill, the other's down below
Everyone is talking 'bout the night he spent in jail
Today he's free, out walking on a million dollars bail
On a million dollars bail

Let Us Now Praise Sleepy John, 2007

The Words in Red

He heft a leatherbound Bible
Up with two hands
Then slammed it down
Over my head
Now he can tell you about
The sins of man
But he must've skipped
The words in red

Love your brothers and your sisters
Take care of each other
Love your enemies
As well as your friends
Tend the poor and the sick
And the ones in jail
Give away your wealth
Say the words in red

Blessed are the meek they'll inherit the earth
Blessed are the wine and bread
Blessed are those that hunger and thirst
Blessed are the words in red

Words in red—words in red
These are the words that Jesus said
Precious words Jesus told
Worth the wait in the world of gold

Now, he's a sinner-huntin' preacher
In the red light zone
At least that's what
The papers said
These finger-pointing fools
Are the first to go
And turn their back
On the words in red

You can call it myth or a church man's dream
You can damn it all from A to Zed
You can bury it deep, you can sell it out cheap
But you can never lose the words in red

Words in red—words in red
These are the words that Jesus said
Precious words Jesus told
Worth the wait in the world of gold

Wig!, 2010

Somebody Told the Truth

The courthouse emptied out
The jurors all went home
The lawyers eased their guilty hearts
The cops were on their own
The soldiers left their camps
The weapons lay in heaps
The generals disappeared
The prisoners were freed, 'cause

Somebody
Somebody told
They told the truth to somebody
Somebody told the truth

The theaters emptied out
The radios went dead
The stadiums were silent
And not a word was said
The dots were all connected
The lines were barely drawn
The secrets night kept hidden
Were left out in the dawn, 'cause

Somebody
Somebody told
They told the truth to somebody
Somebody told the truth

The starving men and women
For once they got their fill
The children of the highway
Were singin' on the hill
The politicians vanished
They must have caught their plane
The clandestine policeman

Were left out in the rain
I sat down on the curbstone
I rubbed my eyes and coughed
I rubbed my wrists and ankles
And I thanked the lord above, 'cause

Somebody
Somebody told
They told the truth to somebody
Somebody told the truth

2005; Wig!, 2010

House Rent Party

She was standing on the corner of wonderland and woe
Waiting for the light to change and wondering where to go
Take the bottles to the grocery? The records to the shop?
Or step out on the sidewalk and make some traffic stop?

'Cause the phone is disconnected
Landlord's at the door
Tow-truck's at the curbside
Here to repossess the Ford

And there's a house rent party tonight, everybody shake
We're gonna blow the roof sky high, see how much
    we can take
When they put you on the street you can sit and watch
    the dawn
But there's always something you can do when you're
    last gold dollar's gone
There's a house rent party tonight

He's in his double breasted jacket, some cherry
    wing-tip shoes
Big 'ol hat with a feather high and a pocket flask of booze
But he can't afford the treatments and there ain't
    another cure
Sad to say without more pay he won't get well no more

Then the night falls up on Broadway
The neon starts to shine
The dancers in the love act
Are gettin' ready for the grind

And there's a house rent party tonight, everybody shake
People come from miles around, now we're gonna catch
    a break

And I know we're gonna make it, don't care what I
    have to do
'Cause I know you'd do the same for me as I would
    do for you

There's a house rent party tonight

So I bought a lucky ticket and I pinned it to the shelf
I put one away for you baby and I kept one for myself
I'm gonna take my winnings, I'm gonna disappear
I'm gonna start a brand new band, we'll play anywhere
    but here

'Cause there's nothing coming in, sugar
And nothing going out
There's nothing left to talk about
If all we do is shout

There's a house rent party tonight, everybody shake
We're gonna blow the roof sky high, see how much we
    can take
When they put you on the street you can sit and watch
    the dawn
But there's always something you can do when you're
    last gold dollar's gone

And there's a house rent party tonight, everybody shake
People come from miles away, now they're gonna catch
    a break
And I know we're gonna make it, don't care what I have
    to do
'Cause I know you'd do the same for me as I would do
    for you
There's a house rent party tonight

Wig!, 2010

All Dressed Up (For Trial)

Put on a worn out suit, an old blue tie
Shined my shoes and said goodbye
Before noon I'll know the tale
Will I go free or back to jail?

I'm all dressed up
I'm all dressed up for trial

Never hurt nobody else
And no one knows the way I felt
Now in the care of a public
Defender says I should cop a plea

I'm all dressed up
I'm all dressed up for trial

The DA throws his weight around
They all assume I'm jailhouse bound
I tell the truth but that won't help
I'm terrified to be myself

They listened in to smoke me out
The court says there's no room for doubt
A witness lied, the jury coughed
The judge got scared she'd look too soft

And I'm all dressed up
I'm all dressed up for trial
All dressed up
I'm all dressed up for trial

The lawyer says there's a railroad down
To prison from my side of town
They saw my face and read my skin
And now they say I'm goin' in

The wheels and gears of justice grind
But justice still gets left behind
So when you see me on the street
You heart don't have to skip a beat

'Cause I'm all dressed up
I'm all dressed up for trial
All dressed up
I'm all dressed up for trial

A higher court will now decide
Who gets judged for real this time

A higher court will now decide
Who gets judged for real this time

A higher court will now decide
Who gets judged for real this time

And I'm all dressed up
I'm all dressed up for trial

HWY 62, 2015

Evicted

We gather here on Christmas Eve
To bid farewell before they leave
On sidewalks painted black with tears
The tenants home of forty years

They built the houses, sowed the trees
Struggled in the factories

Evicted on their way home
Evicted—turned out to roam
Driven from the neighborhood

There are locks and chains on the door
No one lives here any more
Golden light and traffic roars
It's time to wonder what's in store

Money's tight and labor's cheap
But we all need a place to keep

Evicted on our way home
Restricted—turned out to roam

The lawyers and the bankers sigh
Silver teardrops in their eyes

When there was no room at the inn
They wouldn't let their savior in
Now the poor deserve some equity
And not the sheriff's deputy

When our lives are over here
To points unknown we'll disappear

Evicted on our way home
Convicted—turned out to roam

HWY 62, 2015

If I Go Crazy

We had a great big double bed
By a window on the street
We never had much money then
But life and love were sweet
Then we moved to the Hotel Baker
At the corner of Polk and Pine
Rain fell non-stop forty days
And everything was fine

If I go crazy I will lose my mind
Before it all goes hazy, baby
Try me one more time

One summer day in San Joaquin
We hit the county fair
I played my show it was time to go
But something held me there
So we went out to the racetrack
Charmed by an inside tip
I bet everything we had on the
    seventh race
And watched that damn horse trip

If I go crazy I will lose my mind
Before it all goes hazy, baby
Try me one more time

Try me one more time
Try me one more time
Try me one more time
Try me one more time

She rode in on a milkwhite mule
Through the trumpets and the
    cavaliers

Alive to the bright adventure
Of the streets and chased my fears
Now I can talk to anyone
Know what's in their hearts
Go anywhere in the world I want
Even make a brand new start

But If I go crazy I will lose my mind
Before it all goes hazy, baby
Try me one more time

Now the mayor's on a downtown stage
Looking like she's half asleep
The President's on his telephone
Digging himself in deep
But I have got the super-powers
Everybody does
Who ever helped somebody out
And done it just because

Who never answers later
When asked to lend a hand
Who never turns their eyes away
When asked to understand

But If I go crazy I will lose my mind
Before it all goes hazy, baby
Try me one more time

Try me one more time
Try me one more time
Try me one more time
Try me one more time

HWY 62, 2015

Pelican Bay

A convicted full time burglar
Made a prison break
He lasted three weeks on the run
Got as far as the next state

So, they brought him back and sentenced him
To fifteen years of Hell
Sent him to the SHU at Pelican Bay
And a solitary cell

He said, "There's nothing to it"
To himself as they slammed the door
It was an eight by twelve foot cubicle
A bed and not much more

In the Pelican Bay Supermax
No calendar can count the days of
Endless isolation
Lost in a one room maze

There's two million people in prison
Tonight in the U.S.A.
Eighty thousand in solitary
And a hunger strike at Pelican Bay

Day and night—fluorescent light
No window for the sun
They shove your food in through a slot
So you never see no one

It's a twenty-three hour lockdown
Under their control
You never leave, you can hardly breathe
It rots away your soul

There's two million people in prison
Tonight in the U.S.A.
Eighty thousand in Supermax
And a hunger strike at Pelican Bay

He made himself a chess set
Out of blanket lint
But the guards were feeling angry
So they confiscated it

For the slightest of infractions
Extracted from his cell
Pretty soon he's got a broken jaw
And the guards just say he fell

There's two million people in prison
Tonight in the U.S.A.
Eighty thousand in solitary
And a hunger strike at Pelican Bay

It ain't no kind of justice
It's a system of abuse
There ain't no court watching over this
Politicians say what's the use

We have the highest rate of incarceration in the world
Half the prisoners are brown or black
It's a brand of slavery
Everybody knows the deck is stacked

There's two million people in prison
Tonight in the U.S.A.
Eighty thousand in Supermax
And a hunger strike at Pelican Bay

HWY 62, 2015

The Long Good Time

Mother was doing her ironing
While listening to Nat King Cole
Teenagers came and went in cars
All tuned to rock n' roll
Windows were open in the screen door heat
Locusts were buzzing on the summer street
The feelings passed, now I can't recall
How we never thought that we had it all

Everyone, everyplace, everything has been erased
That's the way it goes
First the laughter, then the light, now they're all gone
And locked up tight where the cold wind blows
But we'll all meet again at the end
Of the long good time
We'll all meet again at the end
Of the long good time

Sweet little flowers called snowdrops
In the backyard with the fresh mint leaves
A cherry tree with a rope to climb
And robin's nests under the eaves
My band was playing in the basement
Driving folks out of their minds
Mother called down from the top of the steps
"Boys, play that nice song about suicide"

Everyone, everyplace, everything has been erased
That's the way it goes
First the laughter, then the light, now they're all gone
And locked up tight where the cold wind blows
But we'll all meet again at the end
Of the long good time

The power's cut, the house is cold
The books are boxed, the furniture's sold
Memories drift, our souls drift too
The world keeps turning
What's it turning to?

Me and Pa were circling the table
Fighting the war with our fists
Papa said to Mama, "The boy's insane
There's a viper in our midst"
Years later we made amends
Guess those ribs didn't hurt no more
You could even say we became good friends
When we saw what we had in store

Everyone, everyplace, everything has been erased
That's the way it goes
First the laughter, then the light, now they're all gone
And locked up tight where the cold wind blows
But we'll all meet again at the end
Of the long good time
We'll all meet again at the end
Of the long good time

HWY 62, 2015

Waiting on a Plane

They shut the gate
The inbound's late
There's no one here
I'm trying to get it straight
Ain't going nowhere
I'm waiting on a plane

Flight's been and gone
Next one's at dawn
The tarmac's wet
Night drags on and on
I gave up cigarettes
And now I'm waiting on a plane

I've gone as far as I can go
Until tomorrow
I swear I'll give back what I owe
Everything I stole
I only meant to borrow

Canned trumpets moan
A tune unknown
Fluorescents play
At turning flesh to stone
It's USA today
And I'm waiting on a plane

I've gone as far as I can go
Until tomorrow
I swear I'll give back what I owe
Everything I stole
I only meant to borrow

I think of you
The things you do
I'm gone so much
I know you feel it too
I miss your love and touch
I'm still waiting on a plane

I pace the floor
And watch the door
I never quit
Is that what dreams are for?
Keep the candle lit
I'm waiting on a plane

HWY 62, 2015

Water From a Stone

From Arriaga, Chiapas on a train called the Beast
Trusting our lives to the ones from the east
The coyote dropped us and on the same day
The border guards caught us and they locked us away
We need water
Water from a stone
Living water

A six-year-old child is facing the judge
She can't have a lawyer—the mayor won't budge
They want to deport her though her parents have died
If they send her back now it will be homicide
She needs water
Water from a stone
Living water
Water from a stone

On streets paved with diamonds and gold
You hold your head high but the future is sold
The temperature's rising way up in the sky
This is Indian land, only yours by a lie

Back in the Mission the mural shines bright
But the people who made it were evicted last night
The landlord's raving—it don't make sense
He's running out the tenants and raising the rents
He wants water
Water from a stone
He needs water
Water from a stone

"Give us your restless—your tired and poor
The wretched refuse from your teeming shore"
On your Liberty Statue the words are so clear
Have they been erased now the future is here?

You're making six figures but you owe that on school
You're fiancé's teaching, so everything's cool
Still you can't help but see on your way out to eat
There in another world at the end of your street
You need water
Water from a stone
Living water
Water from a stone

And they need water
Water from a stone
Living water
Water from a stone

Manufacturing sorrow and exporting doom
Tomorrow the cancer arrives in your room
The rent you collected will stay in its box
You'll have more to do than changing the locks
You'll need water
Water from a stone
Living water
Water from a stone

We need water
Water from a stone
Living water
Water from a stone
We need water
Water from a stone

HWY 62, 2015

A Street Singer's Christmas

The year wound out magnificently, days dropping off like chunks of liquor store ice, into the big muddy river of time, drifting away and melting in the raging currents of the holiday season.

I was down at Market and Powell wearing ragged winter hand-me-downs, looking for a place to set my case amidst the streaming current of Christmas shoppers pushing and stomping their way to the next stop, for the next item on their list. I passed the ringing Salvation Army trio, and the finger pointing psycho preacher at the cable car turnaround.

"You! Will! Burrrrnnn!" he screamed, looking right at me. I looked away and kept walking. Same to you, pal, fuck off.

It was cold out, wet, not raining anymore, though it was pouring an hour before. The sky was already getting dark and the day had just begun. I was alone, and had exactly twenty-five cents left from yesterday's busk session. Danny'd been missing lately, since he took off to Hayward with Nicole. He'd been gone about a week.

I hadn't eaten for a day. Something had to happen. Turning right up Powell I walked as fast as possible up to Union Square, set down my case at the entrance, on the corner, and started singing and playing Sleepy John Estes' "Broke and Hungry," bangin' the snaky riff over and over on my Yamaki Deluxe guitar.

A few people tossed quarters as they hurried past, and two winos, who were sitting on a wall farther back in the park, looked up, did a slow double take, then ambled my way. They'd been sharing a bottle of Night Train Express, but it was all gone now. Ahhhh, Night Train. The cheap wine with the beautifully drawn locomotive blazing down a midnight rail on the label. They looked like they'd be glad to get their hands on a quarter or two.

My fingers were cramped from pressing down the metal strings in the cold, the case was open and bare, the little bit of change I'd made so far could barely buy me a pork bun over at Woey Loy Goey in Chinatown, so I considered quitting and making the long trudge through the Stockton tunnel over to North Beach, when here comes John.

John was an old time hippie from up in the Haight. I knew him from around town; he'd been there since before the '67 boom. John had long dirty blonde hair and big ragged side burns. He was wearing a black stove pipe hat, an old fashioned long coat with tails—to protect him from the chill, jeans with piebald patches, and big worn out work boots. He was hauling a trumpet case that day, though I'd always thought of him as a guitar player. We greeted each other in the gloom of the fading afternoon.

"Hey Peter, what's goin' on, man? How you doin' out here? Where's Danny? You feel like sittin' in?" He glanced in my empty case and got the picture. "Today should be a great day, man. Let's team up and go over to the cable car turn around; we'll be shoveling it in down there."

Glad to have a partner, I picked up and we worked our way through the crowd, back down a couple of blocks, to the red bricks at Market.

"Look, Pete, here's the thing out here. You can't play what you want to hear. You gotta play the song you hate the most. Name a song you hate, one you really can't stand."

I didn't answer immediately, and so he went on. "You hate 'Alley Cat,' don't you? Most guys hate that one."

I thought of the cornball Al Hirt standard. "Yeah, I can't stand that."

"Good," he said. "Play along with me and watch this."

We started playing Hirt's cloying, cheesy hit. John took the lead clumsily on the trumpet, and I did my best to back it with the proper orchestral chords.

We hadn't been at it for fifteen seconds when a passing woman shopper threw a handful of change in the box. A man doubled back and put a dollar bill in the case. A small crowd started to gather. Some tourists took our picture, then came forward and put a twenty in. John stopped blowing horn for a second, pulled the bill out and stuffed it into his pocket for safe keeping.

We made thirty-three dollars in the first fifteen minutes.

"The secret, man, is in the song you hate. That's the one that makes the money. Let's keep playing 'Alley Cat.' You gotta keep goin', past where you're sick to death of it. Just keep goin'. Trust me."

I decided to believe him, and we kept playing, and playing and playing some more, 'til I thought I was gonna lose my mind, and my fingers were gonna freeze and break. Money was flying into our case. It was the highest paying session I'd seen out there.

We played 'til the traffic died, until the second-to-last-shopping-day-before-Christmas was over, and, when we finally packed up, we each pocketed nearly a hundred bucks— by far the best day I'd ever had busking.

We ran into Crazy Horse Danny just as we were closing up shop. He'd come back to the city, and came down here looking for me, so we played ten minutes more of "Alley Cat" with him, so he could make some dough too, then we packed it up, and caught the N Judah streetcar up to the Haight, getting off after the tunnel, across from John's Carl Street pad. We decided to celebrate for a while, first stopping at a liquor store, to get some supplies.

Once we got to John's we all went into his music room at the front of the house, sat around the piano with the little Christmas tree on top, and for the rest of the night, we sang the songs we loved.

On The Way To Daly City

It was winter in San Francisco, 1973.

Larry, the trumpet player was in our orbit now. He was from Brooklyn, had once played in some big Broadway musicals before coming West to get clean, away from the NY drug scene. He'd told us about his drug habit; he'd gotten deep into heroin—regularly tying off and fixing up with the rest of the horn section, in the orchestra pit during the Broadway run of *Hello Dolly*, while the conductor stood watch, looking out at the packed theater.

Now he was out here with us, playing the streets in San Francisco, and collecting ATD—"Aid for the Totally Dependent," known by everyone as "crazy pay"—which kept him in a house he shared in Daly City. ATD was a legendary California program, and if you were certified nuts, ATD would pay your bills for the rest of your life. Most of us only dreamt about it, but he had it, and he was slick, really puttin' one over on them with his "crazy" act, and every month when the check came in, Larry cashed it and went on an insane binge.

Larry was short, stocky, and bald. He dressed in brand new, oversized blue jeans, that hung halfway down his ass. The cuffs were rolled up, and he stomped around in big black cop shoes, a black leather multi-zippered motorcycle jacket, and mirrored aviator shades, carrying a trumpet case in one hand and a black briefcase in the other where he kept his pistol, a black .38. I knew it was in there, 'cause I saw him pull the gun once on a bagpipes player.

He was always exasperated, on the edge of flipping out, angry at the world, but the horn was his reason for living, and he was pretty good, when he wasn't too fucked up to play. He played straight New York commercial jazz.

One day, in a coffee house we'd ducked into to get out of the weather, Larry got up and performed "Theme From Exodus" on the piano for me and some guys. It sounded like shit. Digging his hammer-handed phrasing, seeing his hostile grimace behind the shades, and his massacre of the grand melody, we fell out laughing. "Exodus" was his only number on the piano, but an exodus was the response it got from the rest of the audience.

I was out alone busking on Beach Street in the cold early twilight playing as a group of tourists passed me on the sidewalk like I was standing still. I couldn't bear anymore and was about to pack it up when I saw Larry coming up the street from the direction of the Cannery. He spotted me and headed straight over.

"Hey Peter, man, I thought I'd find one of you guys out here. Whatch'ya doin'? This town ain't happenin', it's dead, man, for losers, I wish I was in New York, I'm tellin' ya. Where's Danny, anyhow? Feldman is gettin' me some more work doin' commercials, and it beats this bullshit, man. Hey let's play one, what'd'ya say?"

He pulled out the horn, adjusted the mouthpiece, put it up to his lips, puckered up, and blew a hideous rasping, broken, descending squawk of a trumpet blast. We plowed our way through "Tea for Two," "Kansas City Blues," and gave up halfway into "Hello Dolly." It was pure musical pain, and even with the added head-turning volume of the trumpet, no one cared, no money was ending up in the case.

"This is nowhere, Case, c'mon let's go over to the Haven. I need ya' to drive me, man, I can't drive. I got my ATD check today...."

"Uh huh."

"C'mon man. I'll buy you some soup," he said. "Then you can drive me home. I got room at my place. You can crash there tonight."

He pulled a little bottle out of his leather jacket, poured a few pills into his fist, then with a rapid motion tossed them into his mouth, and choked 'em down, without water. "It's my medicine, I gotta take it, don' look at me like that," he said, and we set off to search for his car.

We couldn't find the car and Larry was cursing. He figured it'd been stolen, and he was gonna kill whoever took it. He began to think his friend, the saxophone player, Feldman, might be responsible.

"That motherfucker! He's a thief, Case. Can ya' believe this shit? I go out of my way to help the guy, and he rips me off!"

I knew that Larry was lucky Feldman was even speaking to him after the outrages that had gone down the week before, but I said nothing. After spending thirty minutes wandering up and down Beach Street, we finally found the car—a little, green, late model VW—parked where he left it, at a 45 degree angle to the curb. It had a parking ticket on the windshield, which he swore at, grabbed, and tossed in with the other junk in his brief case.

We climbed in and headed cross town, with Larry lambasting me all the way with cursed directions, driving advice, and his psycho-social commentary. He'd lay back in the passenger seat, the brief case open on his lap, while official-looking papers fell out onto the floor. He kept wiping his hand over his face, sputtering, and knocking off his own glasses.

"Someday you'll learn, Case. If you wanna be a winner, you gotta act like a winner, dress like a winner, do the things a winner would do."

Every so often, he'd go silent, then he'd lurch up in his seat, turn my way, and do a big double take, like he was noticing me there for the first time.

We got over to the Haven, at California and Polk, and parked. Larry took ten minutes getting out of the car, arranging things in the briefcase, putting them in, taking them out, switching his shades for black horn rimmed glasses. Some of the papers fell out of the open car door and scattered in the street. "Oh, my prescriptions! Peter, help me! Pick those up before they blow away!"

I ran and chased the scraps from the gutter, finally caught them all, brought them back, and handed them to Larry, who didn't say a word but became intent on shoving them back into the pockets of his case. Finally, we left the car and walked towards the restaurant.

The Haven, open 24 hours, was where the all night people congregated for their avocado and sprouts on wheat bread, for their healthy soups, new age salads, and strong coffee—as well as their speed, pot, Quaaludes, and heroin. The place was a combination of low rent health food restaurant and mystical whorehouse. It was dark inside, with the indirect lighting turned way down, and you could sit in the big leather booths 'til dawn if you wanted, and no one seemed to care what you did, as long as you ordered something. The jukebox blared constantly: "My Guy," "Living for the City,"

"Let's Stay Together." The clientele was mostly gay men in their twenties, glittered rockers, drugsters, and nocturnal outlaws. From midnight to six a posse gathered out front, in leather jackets and platform shoes, eye shadow and lipstick, chain-smoking, looking up and down the street, watching out for cops, waiting for the deal to go down. I found this place on my second day in California.

Larry staggered on the way in and collided with a skinny rock and roll kid by the door. The kid snapped, "Watch where you're going, Kojak!" But Larry didn't seem to notice and stumbled on past the cordon-rouge into the service line. The omelet traffic moved slowly, while Larry looked for his wallet, which he seemed to have misplaced.

"Case, that kid by the door, he kipped my billfold! Sonofabitch is a pickpocket!"

I looked up and saw the kid still standing by the door, his back to us, talking to someone with a beehive hairdo and plastic raincoat.

The jukebox was playing "Just Like Tom Thumb's Blues." Larry's wallet was where he'd dropped it, looking like a little dark turd on the floor, a few feet behind us. I went back and picked it up, then stepped forward and handed it to Larry, who was still frantically patting himself down. When he saw the wallet he immediately seized up, then grabbed it out of my hand and reared back.

"YOU! How did you get this? You crooked motherfucker! You stole my wallet? Don't fuck with me, Case!"

As he spoke, his eyes were focused on a spot in the middle of my forehead. Every few seconds they'd dart a quick look down, into mine, meeting my glance for the tiniest of moments, than shifting back up to my forehead again.

"Easy, Larry. Maybe you should try and pay attention to what you're doing."

He glowered at me, pretending he wasn't sure what to believe. Having a hard time focusing, he was looking at everything twice, and beads of sweat began forming on his upper lip. The line moved forward, and soon we were standing by the cauldrons of hot, steaming soups, several big black pots of 'em, on the other side of the glass sneeze guard: minestrone, corn chowder, lobster, and French onion.

"What will you have?" asked the server, but Larry couldn't tell; he needed to make a closer inspection, so he bent over at the waist and reached his head under the glass and over the soups, to get a real good look. His glasses steamed up, then fell off, and landed—plop—in the bisque, floating on the simmering pink surface for a moment, before they sank in and vanished.

He jumped forward and reached his arms into the pot. The server was shouting, the bouncers were on us, dragged us to the door, and pushed us out. Larry was loudly complaining the whole way, "I want my glasses!' His shirt was splashed with soup stains, and his forearms were dripping with the reddish, viscous glop.

We finally got Larry's spectacles back, they were tossed out the door, but not before Larry made a promise to kill the night manager if he ever saw him again. "I'll shoot you, you dirty fop!"

"Shoot yourself," said the man, and we were back on the street.

The freeway south of the city was fogged in, nearly dead, as Larry's green bug hurtled through the orange and grey striped light. Larry had curled up sideways in the passenger seat, facing the door nearly knocked out, mumbling curses and complaints as I drove. The world seemed far away, sort of stuffed, like I was watching it in a diorama. The radio was tuned to cheap jazz, and it sounded strange—kind of muffled, out of tune—and, in fact, everything seemed a little bit wrong, like God had come down and moved the furniture while we weren't looking.

We didn't eat after being bounced from the Haven. I was hungry, but figured the best thing to do was to get the first trumpet here off the street before the window of stoned opportunity slammed shut, and we were really stranded. We just had to get to his pad in Daly City. I was so tired I felt kind of sick myself.

We were about halfway there when the car started to blow it: wheezing, slowing, starting up again. We'd lose power for a second, the lights dimmed and the engine choked, then it began to cough, shake, sputter, race, and whine. I didn't know what was wrong, but I backed off the gas pedal, then jammed it down hard, and after a second's delay, the car blasted something loud out of it's backend, hesitated, lurched ahead, then recovered, and took off; everything seemed fine.

A moment later, the engine completely died, and I had to roll onto the shoulder, where we slowed to a halt. We sat there on the side of the road in the dark, me just staring straight ahead, and Larry now facing me. Everything was quiet except for the whoosh and fade of a passing car.

Larry began to rave: "What'd you do to my car, Case? You killed it. Can't you do anything? Man, I never should have let you drive! Where'd you grow up? Didn't anyone ever show you how to operate a car? I'm ready for Napa! I belong in there, for trusting somebody like you."

The engine wouldn't turn over. I tried again and again, but it just wouldn't go, and the battery was running down. The car sounded desperate, like a tuberculosis victim trying to clear his throat, unable to breathe. One last time, it almost caught on, but after that never got close.

Larry finally shut his mouth and leaned back in his seat, eyes toward the ceiling. He'd gone still and silent, maybe contemplating the seven stages of grief. I was trying to think of something, 'cause until I did, we'd be sitting there.

Who knew what would happen if the cops should stop and come across him in this state? They wouldn't be amused to find his gun, for starters. We had to get out of there, asap. If Larry was still able to walk we could've trundled off and abandoned the car until we found somebody with jumper cables, but one look at Larry told me he wasn't walking anywhere. Whatever he'd taken outside the Haven, as we left, well, it was good.

"Now listen, Larry, there's only one thing to do. I want you to pull yourself together, get out of the car, and come over here, sit in the driver's seat, and steer. I'm gonna get in back and push, get it started down the grade here. Once it gets going fast enough, all you gotta do is let out the clutch and it'll start, then just feed it a little gas, pull off to the side of the road, and let me catch up. Then I'll drive again. Okay?"

That was okay with him, so I pulled on the parking brake and opened my door. I looked over and watched, as Larry opened his door, took a first step out, and disappeared from view. He'd vanished, right in front of my eyes. I sat there blinking for a second,dumbfounded and scared, then I got out of the car and ran around the back, over to his side, calling his name, but he was nowhere in sight. What the hell?

"Hellllp! Peter! Hellllp!"

I looked over the side of the freeway embankment, way down over the steep slope of the gravel, jade plants, and dirt, and spied him—thirty feet down, the top of his head barely visible, floating like a little moon in the dark. He was moaning: "Help me! Help me, Peter!"

I scrambled and slid down the embankment, nearly losing my balance. When I got down there, I found him lying on his back, completely calm now, staring up at the sky and not moving. His eyes shifted towards me.

"I fell," he said.

I started trying to help him up the steep slope, and it was nearly too much. Tugging at his arms, shoving him, I felt his dead weight, and smelled his perspiration and the stale whiff of his breath. We were covered in dirt; my knees and elbows were scraped and sore, both of us breathing like we were drowning, and now it was my turn to curse him: "C'mon, Larry! You fuckin' jerk, you're not even trying! C'mon motherfucker! Get it together!"

"I'm gonna kill you, Peter!"

"You ain't killing nobody, fucker! You can't even walk! Get your feet under you and push!"

With a superhuman effort, and after what seemed like eons, we made it to the top. But then, somehow I lost my balance and Larry loosed his grip, and he tumbled and slid all the way back to the bottom again.

Time froze. We struggled in Purgatory, going on Hell. Finally, as I'd nearly lost my will to survive and was considering just stalking off and leaving him out there for the buzzards and the California Highway Patrol, we made it to the top somehow, onto the level, and I got him into the driver's seat; we were ready to go.

"You know what to do," I said. Then I got in back and pushed as hard as I could; the car wouldn't budge.

I yelled, "Larry! Take off the fucking brake!"

He released the brake, and I got it going down the slight incline, slowly at first, then faster and faster. It picked up speed, but with me still pushing behind. Larry started to veer out into the highway, but just then a semi pulled up through the fog, nearly on top of us, leaning on his horn, AHHHHHHHNK!

"Larry! Argghhhh! Keep to the right!"

He steered it back over to the right, but now he was going too fast for me to keep up. I ran after him as he pulled away, gaining speed down the hill.

"Start it, Larry! Start it now!"

I stopped running, dropped back, and watched as the green VW swerved down the hill, silently coasting, rolling off into the distance.

He made it onto the next exit off the road. I could barely see him now. He was about a quarter mile away, still not starting the car, but just letting it roll down, then up, up, taking the rise, slower and slower, at last coming to a halt right there where the exit ramp started to bend, way up there 'neath the distant haloed streetlights, then, finally it stopped right in the middle of the road.

The taillights were on, everything was silent. Larry was just sitting there with his foot on the brake. I ran to catch up. My heart was pounding but I kept running. The car was motionless. As I got within about twenty feet, Larry opened the door and stepped out. He was standing there, tight lipped, feigning agitation, as if he was pissed off because I was such a moron, shaking his head, his arms up over the open door, just glaring at me, when the car started to roll, slowly, backward, down the grade. The door knocked him down, he fell to the pavement. Just as I got even with the car, the front left tire rolled over his foot.

I jumped into the car, stood on the brake, and stopped it, put it into gear, put on the emergency, and got out. Larry was lying on his back, staring at the sky with the most extremely exasperated expression that I'd ever seen on anyone, anywhere.

He was kind of playing it for laughs.

I helped him off the ground and into the passenger seat, and then got behind the wheel again. I tried the starter, just out of habit, or desperation, sort of an automotive Hail Mary, and the engine started right up immediately, running fine, and we drove over to his Daly City pad.

The place was perfectly middle class with doilies and knick-knacks. Pillows were spruced up on the couch; it was very clean. Home sweet home plaques. A real Norman Rockwell kind of scene. There was a note on the kitchen counter from Larry's roommate saying he'd left town for a while.

Larry told me he was gonna stay up doing something, a high midnight rummaging he needed to do, but I told him I had to crash, and he offered me the roommate's bedroom, saying "Make yourself at home."

Fine. I went in there and sat on the bed. It was an odd feeling after spending a couple of years sleeping in blanket rolls and sleeping bags, to actually be in a bed between sheets. I turned out the lights and felt my way in the dark. The pillows were gigantic. I nuzzled between them like they were two huge, milky white breasts, and sailed away into oblivion.

Hothouse Madman

In the dream of cutting class from Hamburg High, skippin' out on school, I go across the street and into a little record store there on the corner, and start searching through the bin for singles, coming to one that really catches my eye. On a very colorful sleeve, and in wild type, the cover reads Hothouse Madman by the Sergeants. I want to hear the record, but John Lennon is a few feet away, going through records in another one of the bins, and when he sees me with the Sergeants record, he flips out and comes over saying, "I don't want you to listen to that." I say, "Well, I want to hear it." Lennon repeats, "Don't listen to that record!" and tries to grab it from me.

I resist, and carry it over to the counter, and the clerk plays it through the store. It's incredible, a blaring-red, bright, hard-jangle, brand new rock n' roll song.

I wake up and jump out of bed, immediately picking up my guitar to learn it, writing the lyrics from the dream down in a pad, right there on the couch. The chords to the song include some I've never played or even seen before, but my fingers go right to the shapes. The chorus jumps up to a falsetto on "HOT-house madman, hothouse madman." On the guitar solo in the middle of the song, it's rockin' on the low strings. Does it truthfully belong to me? Who knows? But I dig it.

Singing it there in the front room, my friend Elaine listens over and over. She seems to be going for it, and we're both excited and kind of amazed at the nature of the song, and its dreamy inspiration. The music is simple, original, seamless, and goes like crazy. The words are strange, but I feel like I understand them.

"In the dark I'm waiting, near the break of day, crouching in the bushes, when they come my way."

I lay it on the Nerves later that day, after rehearsal over at Pat's. The tune and the chords are sounding great, but everybody's having trouble with the words. Hothouse madman? What's that supposed to mean?

It was always a struggle to fit a new song into the Nerves repertoire. They had to get by Jack, and he was tough, he'd tear them apart. He liked to edit everything down, and in the process disembowel them if you weren't careful. Jack was especially hard on story songs, even ruining some of his own, chopping mercilessly, all in the service of a mad minimalism that almost worked. In some of his songs the first verse repeated three times and that was it. Drummer Paul ratified everything Jack said, as a sort of right-hand man. So it was a gauntlet. I wanted nothing in the world more than to perform my tunes with the band. "When You Find Out" was in. It was undeniable, I guess, a powerful melody and poignant lyrics over a far-out progression of chords that shouldn't work, but did. Jack worked that one over for hours, alone and obsessed down at the end of the rehearsal room, chain-smoking, trying to pry the chords apart, prove that it was somehow put together wrong, but the song was tight and finally he gave up, and the band learned it.

On one of the road trips up the state he told me if I rewrote the lyrics to "Hothouse," we'd do it, and I said okay, great, so as soon as we got back to Hollywood, I went up into my fourth floor digs on Wilton Place and started in on the rewrite.

I set up to work on the kitchen table, with a portable typewriter, some bottles of beer, a stack of paper, some notebooks, and my guitar. Every night I'd take another crack at "Hothouse," knocking off more lyrics to fit the melody, and the hang-up was always the same—the chorus. Nothing seemed to work there, at least not as well as the original. Compared to "Hothouse Madman," every other lyric seemed weak, awkward, contrived. Each day as the sun went down I'd sit at the table for hours and try again, by the open window of summer, listening to the sound of my next door neighbors, The Screamers, having one massive punk rock party after another. I was never really tempted. I could only break the code if I kept writing.

Banging away, version after version, the goal never seemed any closer. After a while, I started writing other songs to break the boredom. "Hothouse" was dead stuck, but "One Way Ticket" just poured out. "In This Town" just materialized as a break from the serious task at hand. I made up nonsense songs, limericks, rock n' roll story songs, blues, getting my writing together without even realizing it. The act of tailoring words in rhythm to the melody of "Hothouse" was so difficult as to be impossible, but was a great exercise. After a spell of that, I felt I could write anything. Anything that is, except a new lyric to "Hothouse Madman."

Here's the original, straight from dreamland:

In the dark I'm waiting
for the break of day
crouching in the bushes
when they come my way

Soon the rose sweet fragrance
tangles with my blood
I wake up when the sprinklers
cover me with mud

There's a vagrant in the garden
they say he means no one no good
I think I better watch out for the
Hothouse Madman
Hothouse Madman
Hothouse Madman
Hothouse Madman

Eat fresh fruit for breakfast
leave the world below
watchdog here in training
he will never know

Why he finds fresh footprints
mornings by the pool
leading to the hothouse
doesn't have a clue

There's a vagrant in the garden
they say he means no one no good
I think I better watch out for the

Hothouse Madman
Hothouse Madman
Hothouse Madman
Hothouse Madman

Life is tasting sweeter
now I'm middle class
living in the suburbs
escaping my past
but listening by their window
I nearly came upset
there's a madman in the backyard
still we haven't met

There's a vagrant in the garden
they say he means no one no good
I think I better watch out for the
Hothouse Madman
Hothouse Madman
Hothouse Madman
Hothouse Madman

The Plimsouls at the Starwood

Some nights, alone in my pad, I'd soar through the early hours of the morning, drunk and stoned, working on songs. Exultation would come over me, a feeling that all the pain and trouble I'd caused were forever in the past, and now I was free. I felt warm, safe, protected, in the arms of the gods.

I'd pass out as the sun came up, waking up a few hours later in the miserable condition I called a "hang-beyond." My head would feel like a dirty glass bowl with fishes swimming around in the murk, and I'd be shaking, sick, terrified, and unable to even get back in bed and sleep it off. I'd be in a cold sweat, and sometimes then the phone would ring and it would be a manager, or an interview, or people at the record company wondering why I'd missed the meeting.

Somehow I'd get through it and make the next gig, to have the laugh of being with the band, then the joy of pouring my heart out on stage in front of mobs of people reveling in the fantastic-ness and excitement of all the noise and soul. Then be home again late, dreaming big dreams in the middle of the night, writing songs and throwin' 'em away, wishing I was on the other side of the universe. Some of the gigs were powerful, but I felt as if I were operating behind enemy lines. I began to get stage fright.

It started like this, one Friday night at the Starwood, one of our favorite clubs. There we are, the Plimsouls, top of the card in front of a 1000 people, 100 degrees, and my anxiety level is building toward the first set for some reason. Before we go on I start really pouring down the screwdrivers, but it isn't working. Beers are lined up on my amp, for insurance, but I have a feeling it's not going to be enough.

My shoes feel wet, loose, hard on my feet. My clothes all of a sudden don't fit. My hands are cold, the guitar strings cut into my fingers, right to the bone. I'm up on the stairs above the stage, in the dark, looking out at the rowdy crowd, the place is going nuts, ready to blow, energy is climbing up my backbone, I have the butterflies, bad, like my guts are turning to water.

I want to run. But our manager Danny is behind me there,

on the landing. He knows I'm nervous, just says, "It's gonna be great." I try to act like that helps. "Yeah." Half of me feels like I'm going to be executed, and the other half is trying to pretend that it's all just good rockin' fun.

Down the stairs and into the mouth of it. I feel shaky, nevertheless, I'm trying to come on bold. The crowd is cheering, Louie's behind his kit now, blam de blam, pish pish blop! Eddie's guitar is a piledriver. I'm fiddling with my dials. Someone's calling out our names, kids looking up, lit by the stage lights, boys and girls, the M.C. yells "Plimmmmmsoooouls!" and we're off into the first song. The lights come up and I go blind with the freight train bearing down on me.

A massive surge of pure electricity courses up my solar plexus. I'm so high, my breath is short and fast, knees weak, shit I'm singing fucking flat. My mouth is kissing the mike ball, I can smell its filth, my mouth is dry, pitching up, and the music is fast white noise. I'm huge now; the world has vanished in the white haze, my body is immense, a house, but I'm trapped, can't get free, a piece of lightning metal sculpture, caught by the nose, by the balls, by my whole life, I turn and wheel back to the drummer, then jerk to the mic where I hold up my leg backward as I sing, still bursting with stage fright, so I'm doing anything I can to elude the spell, making willful mistakes to break the predictability, in hell, shaken, trying to rock my way through it.

We play the tag on "Shaky City" and go into the second song while the audience happily, insanely roars. Drums rolling, tom-toms and maracas, and I'm trying to get some quick beer, from the bottles on top of my amp. We all kick it in.

"Smashing rocks in the burning sun." My mouth is open and a stream of red neon comes out. A loud voice is screaming at me from a few feet away, and I'm lost in a tunnel of brilliant light, alone at center stage. I can't see anybody, just this boiling pitch I'm tossing in. Louie's drums are all that hold me, though, and while the spotlight roves I see the faces at my feet, kids, friends, eyes and mouths, fists; they love it, but they're all caught, just like me.

My strength's returning, my voice is a strip of wet black rubber now, and I disappear into it, sending it out, it's bouncing all over the very back of the room, now to the kids on the stairway. The fear flows away, and I'm left with the size, I'm King Kong on top of the Empire, with the girl in my fist and snapping at planes, now on stiff legs like Frankenstein, colliding with Eddie back at the amps, screaming at the top of my lungs off-mic at Davido who just looks over and laughs at me, then walks away. The crowd is surging back and forth, people look up, out of control with calm eyes, and somebody I haven't seen for ten years is in the front row wearing shades and grinning up at me.

Elvis now. "King Creole." It's a laugh as Eddie solos, a roller coaster and we're riding it, slowly now, between songs, up at the top of the scaffold, about to drop.

Later, the dressing room is a crowded subway train at rush hour. Everyone's sloshing a drink, got their arm around somebody; it's a cocktail party and I'm the guest of honor, so I slip out, make it down the hall, out the back and down the metal staircase, push through the exiting crowd into the parking lot, past the huge line of people waiting for the doors to open on our second show. No one spies me crossing the boulevard, or entering the corner liquor store to score a quart of Mickey's Big Mouth Malt Liquor. Taking the green bottle out in a brown sack, crossing back over Santa Monica, and after taking a quick glance at the pre-show chaos, I traipse on past the club, to the corner, a nondescript office building, then cut into an alley between it and the place behind. There I find several other dark forms propped on the concrete, against the wall, hooded, working on bottles. I plop down, unscrew the lid, and the smell hits me first, like barf, only better. Time for a deep drink.

Soon, I'm more relaxed, almost ready for the second show, so getting up, and nodding a "take it easy" to the guys, I leg it back to the joint. Now the place packed again, more packed than before; somehow they got everybody in. I make it up to the dressing room, now cleared out, and Danny's laughing, yelling at me, "Where you been, man? It's show time!" and this next set goes off crazier and smoother than ever.

Finally, at the end of the night, everyone's gone, and I'm the last to leave the dressing room. I'm going home the same way I got there, sneaker power. It takes about an hour on foot, me still working on a bottle. With a boom box on my shoulder, Smokey Robinson and the Miracles light the way.

Somehow I walk right past my apartment building, as "I'll Try Something New" is playing again. I'm walking aimlessly down Cahuenga Boulevard, when I trip on the curb and nearly fall. The empty streets are cobblestone, and for a second I'm back in Buffalo, over by the train tracks. Tears are in my eyes, I'm crying for my old friends, for the Miracles, for Smokey, for myself, for all the ones who gave everything, so many times, and went down.

A stranger who's been following me at a distance steps out of the dark and pulls a knife. I can barely see through the blur, but I'm pissed. "Fuck off!" I wail at the top of what's left of my voice, and the guy vanishes, just like that.

I come to in my pad on Saturday with an aching head and a worried mind. "We'll be back at the Starwood tonight." Rolling off the bed I reach for a guitar.

Willie Dixon Demonstrates A Style

The great blues songwriter Willie Dixon listened to one of my piano demos at the Bug Music office, and had me over to work at his house in Glendale. It was a little cottage really, a very small place for such a definitive musical giant. His publishing suit against Led Zeppelin for "Whole Lotta Love" hadn't been decided yet. Bug hoped the word on that would be coming soon.

He leaned back in a large leather upholstered chair in his office, peering through bifocals, scratching away at lyrics in pencil on a little pad, with one leg swung up over the armrest, and the other foot firmly on the floor. A parlor grand piano was situated by the front door, in the middle of the adjacent room, in sight of his armchair. He'd ask me to sit down at the keys and pound out infinite repetitions of the two-handed blues groove to the song while he composed lyrics, all based on rhymes for the word smoke. We'd do that for a spell, then I'd come in and we'd discuss music and life.

"Everybody's got to have their own style. Sometimes the name of the style, the song, and the artist are all the same thing—like, Bo Diddley. When I first met Chuck Berry he didn't have a style. One afternoon he came in playing the old country and western song 'Ida Red,' but he had it going a new way, and I told him 'keep doing that so you don't forget it while I set up the microphones,' and that was 'Maybelline'."

"You gotta have your own style..." He starts rummaging over the articles atop a shelf in the back of the office. "I got a style over here for somebody," he says, then turns to me with two harmonicas in his hand, offering one to me and commanding to just "play." He assumed I could, so I did, playing a blues in cross-harp, what they call "second position," the key of G on a C harp, while he lifts the other harmonica up to his mouth and starts wailing a strange lick, a very eerie and keening sound.

It was the first I'd ever seen or heard of a minor harmonica.

"Major against minor," he explained, "that's a style for somebody."

The White House Story

In 2003, I was on a long solo tour of the UK, the Netherlands, and Spain, taking trains from town to town, then a taxi from the train station to the clubs, carrying a suitcase, a guitar, and all my merch, trundling up and down lifts and platforms, jockeying for position in the aisles of moving trains, and up mammoth stairways from subterranean rail tunnels, while all around me rush hour crowds surged and pushed. My whole body ached from the struggle. The tour had begun to feel like an insane sporting event.

In London, I stayed at a one-star hotel off Sumatra Road. Daytimes were spent at an internet cafe doing email interviews for the upcoming tour dates. After three or four question-and-answer sessions in a row, anyone'd get kind of punchy. During an interview for one of Barcelona's dailies, they asked, "What do you think of your president?"

"We need new leadership in the United States, immediately, if not sooner." It's possible that I said a little bit more than that.

These were the Bush years. The Iraq war was killing thousands of innocent people, and was a humanitarian and political disaster.We wrapped up the interview and I headed down the main road, eager to get to my favorite Indian restaurant and enjoy a nice Balti for dinner. But for just a moment, the thought popped into my mind, "Maybe that answer went a little too far." Then I forgot all about it.

The tour in the UK finished, and the next stop was Barcelona for the last leg of the trip.

My Spanish promoters came to the airport and drove me to the gig. They were excited and presented a copy of the newspaper with the interview in it. After the show, I found out that the newspaper was of the political left and the anti-war comments had meant a lot to the audience.

I toured Spain for a little over a week, playing in Madrid, Bilbao, Seville, Majorca, and other spots, then flew to Washington, D.C., rented a car, and checked into a cheap motel on the Beltway. After sleeping off my jet leg, it was time to go out to an internet laundromat.

The first email was from the United States Secret Service

informing me they'd be coming to the Annapolis show, scheduled that weekend at the Ram's Head Tavern. They wanted to have a talk.

I sat there watching my clothes spin in the dryer, while my head spun with anxiety. What the hell was going on?

The next day, I got up and drove three hours through insanely thick traffic to Annapolis. There was barely enough time for a soundcheck. They had me sharing a dressing room with Steve Forbert, who was headlining the show. We had a good time catching up that night, and singing together at the end, Townes Van Zandt's classic song "Pancho and Lefty."

After the show we sold CDs, met folks and signed autographs. There were a number of people waiting to talk. Finally, the place began to empty out. At the very end of the line there was was a fellow wearing khakis and a shirt with the silhouettes of martini glasses. Turned out, this was the Secret Service agent. In rock disguise.

He introduced himself and asked if we could talk. He said he was a big fan, but it was plain from the way conversation was going he wasn't. He described himself as a specialist in anarchy. I didn't have anything to say regarding that. He calmly and good naturally rambled on about his specialty, how he was going down to Florida soon for the G-20. There was no comment to make on that, either. He bought a couple CDs, then handed me his card, which had a picture of a badge on it, and his name, Sergeant James Kowalski.

He said, "If you ever want to visit the White House, give me a call," then turned away and left.

The next few days were open, before I was to head south for more shows. My friend Jeff Campbell invited me to play a special, unlisted concert at his private gallery for friends. Jeff was the organizer of a charity called Hungry For Music, which raised funds to buy musical instruments for disadvantaged kids. It was a popular and successful operation, and they'd given away hundreds of guitars, drums, trumpets and the like.

It was a modest event, me singing on the floor for thirty of so of Jeff's patrons. I played my set, hobnobbed with the guests, had a couple laughs, met some friends, and then everyone split. Sitting there talking with Campbell afterwards, at around ten-thirty at night, in the empty gallery, feeling very relaxed as you do sometimes after a show, I thought of a prank.

"Hey Jeff, wouldn't it be funny to dial the guy's number and leave a message saying I'm ready to go to the White House?"

Pulling the card out of my wallet, I borrowed Jeff's cell phone and dialed. A voice answered on the first ring. I hadn't expected anyone to answer at all after hours.

"Hello. Who is this?" He sounded all business.

"This is Peter Case. I'm ready to go to the White House."

"Where are you?" he asked, without missing a beat.

"I'm on Avenue K, at the Hungry For Music gallery."

"I've got the address. I'll be there in twenty minutes." And then he hung up.

"Campbell! The guy says he's coming here, to take me to the White House. You need to come with me, man. I can't go alone."

Campbell says, "How do you even know the guy's really a Secret Service agent? Maybe he had that card printed up. It does look pretty cheesy."

He had a point. The illustration had kind of a Dragnet vibe. I borrowed his phone again and called Denise in Los Angeles.

"D., how are you doing? Look, it's hard to explain, but this guy here who says he's a government agent is coming to take us to the White House... yeah, right now. I wanted to let you know. If anything happens to us, you'll know what was up."

Denise said okay, though she sounded like she could hardly believe it. I promised to call her afterwards and hung up.

Time passed quickly. We went out front to wait, no idea of what to expect.

The gallery was in a nondescript neighborhood with a bit of outlaw street traffic, deals going down, furtive people coming and going. We were watching the street, when we saw our man pull up to the curb in a late model car.

We went over and got in, me in the front passenger seat and Campbell in the back. There he was, looking very casual. He almost seemed like a different person to me.

Campbell was dressed in black converse high tops, jeans with the knees ripped out, t-shirt under a black leather jacket. Head shaved. I introduced them. Kowalski glanced back at Campbell, then over at me and asked, "Is he cool?"

"Yeah, he's cool."

We pulled out from the curb into traffic. I immediately noticed a police cruiser behind us with the lights going. He's pulling us over.

My first thought was, they've set us up. Looking back at Jeff, I saw panic in his eyes. There was a burst of acute pain in my back, a sensation I often get in tight situations.

But our driver just said, "Don't worry about that."

We continued down the street with the cops gum-balling behind us, then finally shutting their lights off and making a right turn.

We made our way across Washington, past the Vietnam War Memorial, and began to see the White House in the distance. It was like being on an LSD trip. Was he really who he said he was? And who was that again?

We pulled up to a fence on a huge parking lot. There was a gatehouse with guards inside. Our driver said a few words and the barrier-arm lifted up to let us through. We drove fifty yards and were stopped by a guard with a bomb-sniffing dog. The guard checked out our driver, while the dog sniffed the car, and then waved us through.

The White House was looming very close, right on the other side of a fence and gate. At a guardshack, with a sentry inside, our driver showed some ID, shared a brief word with him, and once more we were let through, onto the White House grounds. He parked us in a spot about forty feet from the door, and we all got out.

"That's the Situation Room," said our guide, pointing at a row of windows.

At no point had they checked us for identification or even said our names.

We entered, walking along downstairs, then went outside into the Rose Garden, continuing around to the side of the building in the dark.

"That's where the president lives," said Kowalski.

We looked up at the third floor, and saw a dull blue light flickering on the darkened curtains.

"What's he doing now?' I asked.

"He's probably reading some reports," came the answer.

We went back inside and climbed a stairway to the second floor. There was a photo of the president and vice-president in a motorboat, pulling in a gigantic bass with a net. They looked like they were having fun. I studied the photos on the wall as Kowalski spoke to a guard at a podium at the top of the stairs. Once again, no credentials were ever asked of us. We went up the stairs and entered the White House press room. There were rows of wicker chairs, all empty. Our guide pointed out the room where the Cabinet met, and next thing we were standing looking into the Oval Office. The time was eleven o'clock at night. Everyone had left. The Oval Office had the aura of a national historic monument. It was hard to imagine any work being done there. The place seemed for show, with the feel of a million feet tromping through, tho' it was spic and span. The rug seemed kind of worn.

We were standing behind a velvet rope which blocked our entrance. We could see the whole room. Kowalski was going on like a tour guide saying, "When the eagle on the front of the desk is facing left, it signifies a war-time president ..."

I was looking in and thinking, "What would Allen Ginsberg do? We're here, we should exorcise it!" I began saying prayers of purification and protection under my breath. Campbell was right behind me.

"I feel sick," he whispered. "I think I'm gonna throw up."

Kowalski was oblivious, chattering on how the executive office building was the safest place to be in Washington in the event of a nuclear blast.

He showed us around for another ten or fifteen minutes, spouting right wing platitudes all the way, and then it was time to go.

He drove us back to Campbell's neighborhood, and offered to walk us inside.

"No that's okay, man, when a guy gets to be around fifty he can take care of himself," I cracked, but he got out of the car and followed us in, anyhow.

Hungry For Music had a long narrow office, with counter space all the way around. The walls were filled with posters and mementos, and the counters were covered in business related papers, correspondence, orders and such. Kowalski slowly went around the whole room, giving everything a good once over, while he kept up a lightweight banter.

When he'd seen all he wanted to, he said goodnight and split, and that was that, for a while.

The whole thing was confusing. What was happening? Denise and I talked it over on the phone. We had no idea, but certainly, something weird was going on, and yes, it did make me feel a bit wary of communications with the world at large.

Continuing on the road south, the shows in Charlotte, Chapel Hill and Atlanta all went without a hitch. My friend in Atlanta, a book store owner and publisher, listened to my tale one night over coffee, then proceeded to tell a similar story he'd heard.

At the end of his tale, he looked across the table at me, smiled, and said, "You're being investigated."

It'd been six or seven months since the White House trip, when I was booked back into the Washington area, to perform a solo show in Arlington, Virginia, at a popular coffee house. The crowd was out front, milling about, and I was in the dressing room getting ready, when the door swung open and I was standing face to face with the Secret Service agent once again.

He laughed and said, "Hey man…"

He was in his black leather jacket mode, and had his hair slicked back. Every time I saw him he looked different.

"Hey Peter, so, what's the James Brown story?"

I had no idea what he was on about, and said so.

"Yeah you do… what's the James Brown story?"

"Look man, I don't know… but I've got to go onstage now. Give me some room back here, ok?"

He left to go out front, and when I got on stage, there he was sitting right at ringside looking up at me, accompanied by a woman, who seemed likely to be an agent as well.

I tried my best to ignore them, and got on with the work at hand, playing my songs.

Halfway through the set, I got a chill, goosebumps down my arms and back. The James Brown story was coming back.

The "James Brown Story" was the name of a very obscure piece of press material put together in 1979 by a publicist friend of the Plimsouls, before we'd even recorded our debut record. It described the first meeting of the band members in a traffic jam, while they were blasting "Cold Sweat" on an eight-track tape player.

I didn't have a copy of the press release, and hadn't thought about it for years. It had never come up.

After the show, I found Agent Kowalski out near the bar.

"I remembered the James Brown Story. How did you know about that?

"Peter, you can find out everything there is to know about someone, if you're willing to look at Nexus long enough."

When some fans approached to talk, he stepped outside the club. I caught up with him out there.

"Are you investigating me, or what?"

He looked back at me, smiled, then pulled back his leather jacket to reveal a pistol, a service .38, riding in a shoulder holster.

"No, you're just paranoid."

Green Notebook

Rental car

A temporary steel and glassworks friend—rubber and plastic rules the road—silver sleek and that new car smell—clean and ether-esque—while my old ride at home sits by the curb and munches grass on the berm and feels the aches and pains of one hundred and fifty thousand miles—my rental waits for me in its youthful glory—the trunk enjoys the feel of the luggage packed in—the mirrors are set to my size and height as I scan the road behind me—a dependable, big, shiny, gas burning, carbon producing steed, my chariot, my ticket, people look like their cars said Louie, but these are agency wheels out on business and covered by insurance—it blinks its lights when I arrive, like a good dog—when I step on the accelerator there's a moments hesitation before the crouch and rocket—and on the highways—millions of cars, the non-stop river of steel, the trucks in fleets and formations like the supply lines of an endless war—troops and provisions always being sent to the front—the wounded and dead returning—we're living on the battlefront everywhere we go—my car, its cab a refuge on my long and trickier days of distance and time, the occupations of a tavern singer.

12 hour turnaround

After navigating the freeway and a service road—then, a crowded motel office—now crossing the parking lot with luggage—two trips with arms clinging to instruments and clothes—the next door neighbor eyes you suspiciously—is that hostility in his eyes?— the door clicks behind—the light is felt for, fingers do the walking in the dark—and they come on—the air is dry and a chemical cleaner's been used—the room is chilly—there is one thin garishly colored cover for the bed—orange and blue—and from experience you know the heater will either misfire or fry the cords—but now's the time without having to keep an eye cocked at the highway—to close your eyes and fall into inner space—play some music through the tiniest of speakers—reading—writing—'rithmetic—the little stale schoolhouse—drinking lots of water—in this sanctuary the near-by highway is a steady roar—gotta get some sleep so I can drive tomorrow but it's so much fun just being in this dump alone and not moving.

Jumbo

Discolored from rain on the tarmac near Detroit—TSA left the snaps half undone—and now it looks bruised—the old jumbo twelve string—called it "the cannon"—it's loud and deep—feels alive in my hands—a sound to express the american red brick honky tonk beauty I began to hear 1970 or so—the twelve string is a spiritual instrument—I said it for laughs but it's got a lot of truth to it—the thinner octave strings suggest another parallel dimension—the realm that follows and corresponds to this one—the plonk and jangle—the boom and chime—quicksilver brightness—the deep notes with their higher twins—cutting through the air—through depression, despair and boredom—through objectivity and abjectivity—all twelve strings are extra arms in the fight for light—harder to bend—but more worth it—still pliant—making the most of a simple phrase—twelve gates to the city—my protector—a wall of sound?—blues on the twelve—Hendrix—Leadbelly—McTell—Pete Seeger—it's heroic—I saw John Hammond Jr. at McCabe's that night on a guitar just like his one—maple—blonde—tuned way down to see—needs to be treated with blessings, gratitude and respect.

Morning

The first breeze of the new day and a glow enters from the east—I feel the whole country light up like a giant map—I know they've risen in Virginia beach —are manning their stations in St. Louis—the first draws of day as the world spins you out of bed and into the half-light—I have an operation on my heart in the morning—this could be the last dawn I'll ever see—but it isn't and I'm in the I.C.U. by eleven A.M.— the world caterpillars forward incessantly the scrunching and stretch and slight retreat—this time breakfast comes up short—coffee and a cube—with a splash of white—my eyes are sticky and need a splash of their own—my body is crying to lay back down and retreat—the coffee was brewed and stretches are attempted dizzy looking for my sneakers— this is the day the Lord made and could contain the big phonecall—the diabolical crash—the sweetest kiss—a commendation—the lovers hand—unexpected recognition and love or grief—the morning doesn't blush—isn't shy—is young but self assured—moves forward through all without a doubt and never looks back—has a few secrets—but knows what's hidden by force of the little sparrows who peep at the cafe table for some bread crumbs and the dog who shakes her head.

San Francisco

Vistas of natural beauty—the bay and the ocean—the opposite shore seen clearly or hiding in the mist—the golden red gate—the wheeling seabirds and the shining traffic—when I first got here I saw lineaments of the old wild west—the view over hills of three story buildings and roofs of vintage SF style to the cathedral on top—a snail crawling and cresting the hill with its two big horns—so sight lines figure large—the density of life—the people all together— Chinese and Russian and Black Americans and Latinx— the neighborhoods are fading—but the Mission is still the Mission, North Beach continues—the Haight is a ragged mall but still a center for outlaws and drifters—the Fillmore is the most changed and destroyed from what it once meant as a black neighborhood and now it's high end shops and people doing their pale and scaredy thing—up close over coffee and the walks and shops—still some singers on the street—still some poets in the Mission—sometimes you even see people in love—there has been an exodus—ghosts parade the public spaces—everywhere I look I see shadows and everybody's closer here—packed into seven square miles—reverberations and percussion—and over and under it all—a cloud of political corruption and big money—the giants—"save our city."

Denise

I've known her since the early eighties—one or the other of us was always in a marriage—but after a first mysterious and stormy incident no one quite recall the details of— it was love at first sight—a long story—she came backstage to meet me in Atlanta—on the Blue Guitar tour—she was so beautiful—dark hair and deep brown eyes—she's my angel but we met up again a few days late—fate wanted us both to weather the nineties in other ways I guess—but I always knew she was out there. Denise taught me about love—I trust her all the way—she can write—we've been together twenty years and can still talk all night—I'm not playing loose with her love—it's my only earthly treasure—we've been through an emergency or two—soldiered through a couple of low Karma seasons—but even then we keep laughing—if she decides to do something it's enough for me that she wants it—my only regret is we can't be young together again—but today is life and freedom is what you can do—sometimes we feel ground down—boxed in by living on the outlaw side of a culture that doesn't accept mistakes—nevertheless—she brings me her gift of love—and a way of getting into the action—the center of the heat—justice for all—in black and white—speaking the truth from our beautiful gospel crib and broadcasting it up into the tower—hope she likes her portrait!

Evening

Birds are calling from darkening trees as the air cools and lights begin to shine golden from the houses—the tiles of the roofs fade into the black sky—televisions in living rooms all focused on the same channel—a man is grimming in black and white—food smells from the kitchen someone likes garlic—the floor is gritty to bare feet—unswept and roughing up the tender toes—a gate is cribbing the back room and its toys—a piano relaxes unplayed the avenues are lit by electric bulbs from above—creating halos over us onto the ground—the heat of the day begins to fade from our skins— the sidewalks are crowded now—the restaurants sit down to a good meal—the nail shop shines like a broadway play—the police round on the stragglers and guard the storefronts—a dog is barking at sailors—who, knowing that it will soon be night are drinking away their leave—the ships sail at dawn and only a few pace the iron decks—the sun keeps setting over and over—it's always evening then night—I write these notes with a dog at my feet.

Space Monkey

Space Monkey, Space Monkey
What you doing out there?
Why, it's dark as a dungeon way up in the air

Come gather round me, you little monkeys, and a story I'll tell
About a brave young primate, outer space knew him well
He was born at the top of a tall swaying tree
Back in the year 1953

He could swing through the jungle and hang by his toes
But they took him to Russia cause they could, I suppose

Space Monkey, Space Monkey
What you doing out there?
Why, it's dark as a dungeon way up in the air

They dressed him up in a spacesuit and it started to snow
Shot him up in a rocket where no man would go
He whirled and he twirled as he flew through the sky
He got kind of lonesome but space monkeys don't cry

Space Monkey, Space Monkey
What you doing out there?
Why, it's dark as a dungeon way up in the air

He had Cuban bananas and plenty of Spam
But he couldn't figure out how to open the can
One day he slipped on a banana peel and the ship lost control
It spun out of orbit and shot out a black hole

Now it's been four decades, that's nine monkey years
A long time for a monkey to face all his fears
For a little space monkey life just isn't fair
And it's dark as a dungeon way up in the air

Space Monkey, Space Monkey
What you doing out there?
Why, it's dark as a dungeon way up in the air

Now Leningrad is Petersburg and Petersburg's hell
For a card-carrying monkey with a story to tell
There'll be no one to greet you when you get back home
No hammer or sickle, you'll be all on you own

Space Monkey, Space Monkey, it's time to get real
The space race is over, how does it feel?
Cold War's had a heatwave, Iron Curtain's torn down
They've rolled up the carpet in Space Monkey Town

Space Monkey, Space Monkey, there's no one to blame
Like the dog who flew Sputnik, your career's down
    the drain
Space Monkey, Space Monkey, there's nothing to do
But it's better than living in a Communist zoo

Space Monkey, Space Monkey
What you doing out there?
Why, it's dark as a dungeon way up in the air

(John Prine, Peter Case)

John Prine, Live on Tour, 1997

Discography

The Nerves EP, 1976
Zero Hour EP, The Plimsouls, 1980 (Beat Records)
The Plimsouls LP, 1981 (Planet/Elektra)
Everywhere at Once, The Plimsouls, 1983 (Geffen Records)
Peter Case, 1986 (Geffen)
The Man with the Blue, Postmodern, Fragmented, Neo-
    Tradionalist Guitar, 1989 (Geffen)
Six Pack Of Love, 1992 (Geffen)
Sings Like Hell, 1993 (Vanguard)
Torn Again, 1995 (Vanguard)
Kool Trash, The Plimsouls, 1997 (Shaky City/Fuel 2000)
Full Service, No Waiting, 1998 (Vanguard)
Flying Saucer Blues, 2000 (Vanguard)
Thank You, St. Jude, 2001 (with David Perales)
    (Traveling Light/Prima)
Beeline, 2002 (Vanguard)
Bomblight Prayer Vigil, 2006 (Verb, CD Issue Two)
Let Us Now Praise Sleepy John, 2007 (Yep Roc)
Wig!, 2010 (Yep Roc)
The Case Files, 2011 (Alive)
HWY 62, 2015 (Omnivore)
The Midnight Broadcast, 2020 (Bandaloop)
Doctor Moan, 2020 (Bandaloop)

Index of Titles and First Lines

Peter Case

Lifelong musician, wrote first song in 1965, learned to play on the streets of San Francisco, founding member of punk rock precursors the Nerves, lead singer of the Plimsouls, solo singer since 1984, twelve solo albums since 1986, three Grammy nominations, a few thousand gigs on four continents, hundreds of songs, rock and roll, surrealistic-documentary love songs, deep hymns and blues, various topical, prophetic poems, prayers, and incantations, with melodic outreach, on piano and tuned, detuned and re-tuned six and twelve string guitar.

In memory of

John Prine

1946-2020

Made in the USA
Monee, IL
22 November 2020